Just JavaScript:
An Idiomatic Approach

First Edition

Ian Elliot

I/O Press
I Programmer Library

Ian Elliot, Just JavaScript: An Idiomatic Approach
1st Edition
ISBN Paperback: 978-1871962574
First Printing: April, 2018
Revision: 0

Published by IO Press   www.iopress.info
In association with I Programmer   www.i-programmer.info

Preface

Most books on JavaScript compare it to class-based languages such as Java or C++ and often go on to show you how to make it look like the one of these.

Just JavaScript is an experiment in telling JavaScript's story "just as it is" without trying to apologize for its lack of class or some other feature. The broad outline of the story is very clear, but some of the small details may need working out along the way - hence the use of the term "experiment".

Read on, but don't assume that you are just reading an account of Java, C++ or C# translated to JavaScript. You need to think about things in a new way.

Just JavaScript is a radical look at the language without apologies.

It isn't a complete introduction to JavaScript and isn't for the complete beginner to programming. It has been written for those who are familiar with the basic constructs used in any programming language and have already encountered JavaScript.

Initially it looks at the ideas that originally motivated the JavaScript approach and can be considered "pure" JavaScript. Over time, pure JavaScript has been modified and expanded. While these additions haven't broken JavaScript they make it more difficult to appreciate and understand the core principles of the language. On the other hand, you need to know about them to make best use of modern JavaScript. As you proceed through the book you'll find some sections, and even chapters, with "advanced" in their title and this signals that they require you to know more JavaScript than has already been introduced in this book. You can, of course, leave these sections until the complete picture has been presented.

My hope is that by the end of this book you will have a fuller understanding of why and what JavaScript is and can appreciate its differences as strengths rather than shortcomings.

I would like to thank Kay Ewbank for paying attention to the detail of this book and removing many errors. As always, any errors that remain are my own.

Ian Elliot
April 2018

This book is a revised and updated version of the series of *Just JavaScript* on the I Programmer website:

www.i-programmer.info

To keep informed about forthcoming titles visit the publisher's website:

www.iopress.info

This is also where you will also find errata, update information to keep up with changes. You can also provide feedback to help improve future editions of **Just JavaScript**.

Table of Contents

Chapter 4
The Object Expression

Chapter 5
The Function Object

Chapter 6
Functions – Scope, Lifetime and Closure

Chapter 13
Property Checking   **203**

Chapter 1

JavaScript – Essentially Different

JavaScript is a standout language in the current landscape of popular languages. It just isn't like the other languages. This causes a big problem because programmers who have become used to the standard, almost obligatory, approach to programming – object orientation – find it deficient in all sorts of ways. This means they not only misuse it, they also criticize it unfairly.

JavaScript is not Java

nor is it any other class-based, object-oriented language.

In this chapter we look at how we got where we are today and how JavaScript is different in very general terms. The rest of the book focuses on how it is different in very specific terms.

Why would you want to know about this outlier language? Surely it would be better to ignore it and preferably replace it with something more normal, more standard?

Even if, once you fully understand it, you still hate JavaScript, your encounter with it will have made you a better programmer. Rather than accepting the wisdom that has been handed down to you an encounter with a different way of doing things will have given you the perspective you need to come to your own conclusions. However, don't confuse this enlightenment with simply rejecting JavaScript because at first sight it is an inadequate language by conventional standards.

Putting this another way, an encounter with aliens might make you understand humans rather better.

JavaScript's Tortured History

You probably already know the history of JavaScript but you probably haven't appreciated how remarkable it is.

Brendan Eich was employed by browser maker NetScape to create a scripting language. Eich wasn't a typical hacker of the time – he had a degree in computer science and mathematics. So when he was asked for a scripting language he didn't think of modeling it on down-to-earth things like VBA or some other dialect of Basic, he thought of implementing something similar to

Scheme. In case you don't know, and yes Scheme is a little obscure, it is a dialect of the programming language Lisp and heavily functional rather than object-oriented. In short Eich picked what most would consider to be an academic language and not the sort of language that a script would be written in.

However, while Eich was contemplating Scheme, NetScape had its eyes on Java for purely marketing reasons. At the time Java was the next big thing that would save the computing industry. As a result Eich's bosses insisted that the scripting language had to be like Java.

Forced away from his initial design decision, Eich decided to mix Scheme with another little-known language, Self. This made the language share some of the characteristics of Java, at least superficially, and made it more object-oriented than a pure Scheme implementation would have been. Initially the language was called Mocha and it was implemented in just ten days - an amazing feat and admittedly one that probably resulted in some bad choices that we have been putting up with for a long time.

The final thing that the NetScape bosses did to confuse the issue was to change the name from Mocha, which had an implied coffee and Java reference, to LiveScript and then finally to JavaScript, with a more than obvious reference. This is a very sad choice because JavaScript has nothing much to do with Java and it is so much more than a Scripting language.

It also creates a problem about what we call JavaScript to this day. Back in the day when Java was new and was the property of Sun, the name JavaScript was registered as a trademark along with lots of Java related names:

```
   .  .  .
JavaScope(TM)
JavaScript(TM)
JavaServer(TM)
JavaSoft(TM)
JavaSpaces(TM)
JavaSpec(TM)
JavaSpin(TM)
   .  .  .
```

When Oracle took over Sun it acquired the trademark and this is the reason why, when Ecma International (formerly European Computer Manufacturers Association (ECMA) got involved in standardizing JavaScript, it decided to not risk using JavaScript and called the language ECMAScript instead, so confusing everyone in the process. To this day beginners are puzzled by the JavaScript/ECMAScript split. It really wasn't a good move in the first place to use a name for a language that was trademarked by someone else.

JavaScript was implemented on all of the popular browsers with differences that were enough to cause problems. In 1996 Netscape asked Ecma International to standardize the language and in 1997 the first ECMAScript standard, ECMA-262, was produced. This roughly corresponded to JavaScript 1.3. Work continued to ECMAScript Edition 3 in 1999, which essentially defined JavaScript 1.5.

Work stalled on ECMAScript 4, mainly because Microsoft continued to develop JavaScript in its own way. In-fighting between different JavaScript factions led to a slow and non-uniform development of JavaScript, which made lots of problems for programmers. Essentially if you wanted your program to work in a range of browsers, you restricted yourself to an earlier version of JavaScript and implemented feature testing to get around some of the unavoidable differences.

It took until 2009 for the pressures to produce a more modern and standard JavaScript resulting in version 4 being skipped and version 3.1 being renamed ECMAScript 5 – so putting the unhappy attempts to create ECMAScript 4 behind us. ECMAScript 5 and various versions of JavaScript 1.8 are generally considered "classic" JavaScript.

After this things became a bit more difficult again but eventually ECMAScript 2015 was released and this can generally be considered the first modern version of JavaScript. It also marked the switch from arbitrary version numbers to dates – but ECMAScript 2015 is still often referred to as ES6 or ES2015. This also marks the point at which JavaScript version numbers start to lose their meaning, from here on they are either ECMAScript 2015 or they are not.

Following on from ES2015 is ES2016, which introduced a small number of important features and ES2017, which is a minor update compared to ES2015 or 2016. We are promised updates at yearly intervals and, as most programmers think that the language is nearly feature-complete, these are likely to be small changes.

From here on, we will refer to ECMAScript 5 as ES5 and ECMAScript 2015, also known as ES6, as ES2015.

As of 2012 all modern browsers, ones still being developed, support ES5.1. Legacy browsers support ES3, but with a large range of variations notably in the IE series of browsers. ES2015 and ES2016 represent modern JavaScript and they are not 100% implemented in all browsers at the time of writing.

If you didn't live though the difficulties of writing JavaScript that would run on the majority of browsers, you can tell from the history that development wasn't fun. In fact, if you want to support legacy browsers, it still isn't. However, as already mentioned, there is a core of classic JavaScript that not only represents what you can do on the majority of browsers, but also encapsulates the essence or philosophy of JavaScript and this corresponds to ES5.

What Is Special About JavaScript?

JavaScript is often unfairly treated by programmers simply because its name provokes certain expectations. As already stated, JavaScript isn't like Java and it isn't a scripting language. Of course, both of these statements are shorthand for more complicated thoughts.

JavaScript is a bit like Java in that it has similar control structures – for loops and if statements – but then so do most languages. Java's way of doing control was influenced by C and so you could just as well credit C for JavaScript's control statements.

More importantly JavaScript adopts an approach towards objects and types that is radically different from Java. As a result the expectation that JavaScript is Java leads to confusion and disappointment. You will find lots of criticism of JavaScript that essentially reduces to "Java does it better". This is undoubtedly true, as there are many things that Java does that JavaScript doesn't even attempt to do.

Comparing JavaScript with Java is simply a misunderstanding.

In the same way comparing JavaScript with almost any language that takes the same approach – C#, C++ or Python say – is equally flawed.

Most of the rest of this book is about exploring the JavaScript way of doing things but it is worth explaining the general differences between JavaScript and the other popular languages. If you don't understand the points, don't worry as they are explained and expanded later in this book.

First we need a quick overview of the dominant approach to the problem of organizing programs and programming. If you don't know about class-based, object-oriented programming, this will only give you the flavor. If you do know about class-based programming then read the section because it might make you see it in a slightly different light.

Class-Based, Strongly-Typed

Most modern languages in common use today take a single approach to programming which can be roughly summed up as class-based, object-oriented programming.

An object is an entity that has properties and methods. Methods can be regarded as properties that just happen to be functions, so all you really need to say is that objects have properties.

Most languages make use of the idea of a class to create an object. A class is like a specification for the object, i.e. what properties it offers, and once you have the class you can create as many copies of the object as you need.

In class-based programming you first create a class and use this to create an object. This is a good way to work when you want multiple instances of a class, but the fact of the matter is that many of the classes you create are instantiated only once. This means you have problems with names – the class has to be called, say, CSort and the object you create is, say, sort. If you ask a beginner what is confusing they will often say that the need to define a class, when all you need is an object is puzzling. It doesn't matter how much you know that it isn't, you should always listen to what a beginner says is hard to understand, because it usually is where the unnecessary complexities lie.

The class that creates or instantiates an object is also regarded as the object's type. This leads on to the whole idea of strongly-typed languages where what you can do depends very much on the object's type and this is enforced at compile time.

Strong typing is claimed to reduce errors in programs, but there is very little hard evidence that this is the case, no matter how reasonable it may seem. There is little doubt that it does catch errors. If you have programmed using a strongly-typed language, you will have plenty of examples where strong typing has saved you from trying to use a property that an object doesn't have. However, this isn't a difficult trick to pull off in other ways.

The class that is used to create an object is its type, and its type guarantees that the object has all of the properties that the class defines. If you pass an object to a function that is expecting an object of ClassA and the object is ClassB, then strong typing will detect a problem and refuse to compile the program. The reason is that ClassB doesn't necessarily have any of the properties of ClassA and so trying to use them would result in a runtime error. Of course, you might know that ClassB does have the properties and no such runtime error will occur. This doesn't matter, strong typing forbids it so as to protect you from errors.

The point is that strong typing does protect you from errors, but they are the easiest of errors to spot and this isn't the only way to do the job.

The classical theory of object-oriented programming is that the classes you create mimic some sort of real world hierarchy. The usual example is of different types of animal. You start off with a class called Animal and then, using inheritance, derive a Dog and a Cat class from it. Inheritance is a way of creating new classes based on existing classes. The Dog and Cat classes have all the properties of the Animal class and any of their own that need to be added.

Inheritance creates a class hierarchy. As class also defines type, it also defines a type hierarchy. That is, a Dog and a Cat are both examples of Animals. This is upcasting - they can be regarded as of type Animal as well as of type Dog and Cat. When you treat a Dog or a Cat as an Animal you can only use the properties of Animal. To make use of the extra properties you have to cast to Dog or Cat – this is downcasting.

Getting confused? If you are not used to these ideas they are confusing and being confusing to a beginner suggests that they might not be quite as good an idea as experts believe they are.

Class and type hierarchies are never as neat in the real world as in examples. As a result, many class-based, strongly-typed, object-oriented programs tend not to implement their own hierarchies. The reason is that while libraries such as graphics and GUI implementations often have a strongly hierarchical organization based on inheritance, small programs that make use of such libraries don't, because they just do one thing.

This is only a scratching of the surface of the philosophy and approach that has grown up around class-based, strongly-typed languages such as Java. It is not to say that they are all bad or ill-conceived, but they are just one way of approaching the problem of creating programs. You cannot simply judge a language as bad because it doesn't do things in the same way as Java or any other representative of the approach.

Scripting

What exactly is scripting?

A very good question, and there isn't a single answer. A scripting language is generally thought to be something that binds other objects together. It is what you add to an existing system to allow a programmer to add automation features to an application, say. In the case of JavaScript, the existing system is the web page and the objects are the entities displayed on the web page. You can regard JavaScript as a scripting language, but in practice it goes beyond this – although this is a matter of opinion. If you compare JavaScript to languages such as Shell, MS-DOS batch, even VBA, then modern JavaScript is a more developed language. It has features that go well beyond what is needed to simply work with existing objects.

You could regard JavaScript as a language that just happens to have HTML and its incarnation in objects, the DOM, as its UI. Just as Java has Swing or JavaFX, so JavaScript has HTML. Just as no one would reasonably call Java a scripting language, it is equally unreasonable to call JavaScript a scripting language.

Why does this matter?

Partly because the use of the term "script" is belittling and used as a way of not treating the language as worthy of attention. After discovering that JavaScript isn't the same as Java, you can dismiss it as just a scripting language. Nothing could be further from the truth.

Sophisticated JavaScript

The critics of JavaScript make use of the fact that it isn't Java and is a scripting language to avoid having to consider that way that it does things and the possibility that it might be logical in its own way. They use the short time that Brendan Eich had to create the language as evidence that it is a crazy half thought-out collection of hacks.

It isn't.

It is the descendant of Lisp, Scheme, Self and other languages that took a sophisticated and different approach to programming and it is worth understanding.

This glowing recommendation doesn't mean that JavaScript doesn't have its shortcomings. In the well known idiom, it has its bad parts – and some of these are due to its rapid design in its infancy. Interestingly these bad parts usually aren't the bad parts that are identified in the literature. They only become apparent when you understand the logic that drives JavaScript and how occasionally it isn't fully adhered to.

So What Is JavaScript's Approach?

After explaining the approach taken by other popular languages and saying that JavaScript is different, it seems to beg the question what exactly is the approach that JavaScript takes?

This is really the question that the rest of the book answers, and so you can hardly expect a full answer in a few paragraphs. However, an overview is in order.

JavaScript isn't a class-based language. It provides facilities to create objects directly. This makes getting started with object-oriented programs easier. If you want a dog object, you simply implement it – no need to create a Dog class and then instantiate a dog, just create the object you need. This reduces the number of names you need to invent.

Not having classes means that you need another mechanism to implement inheritance and a way to create duplicates of an existing object. JavaScript uses the idea of the prototype to implement something like inheritance and in its earlier incarnations it doesn't do this job as simply as it might.

It also uses the idea of a constructor object to make it possible to create multiple instances of an object, and this too had its problems in the early days of the language. Generally speaking, JavaScript uses the idea of an object factory – an object that creates other objects – to replace the idea of instantiating a class.

You could say that JavaScript's object-oriented approach is centered on using the prototype object and the constructor object to create new objects.

This is something we will have to look into in much more detail.

The other big idea in JavaScript is often summed up as "functions are first class objects".

In other languages it is often the case that, for reasons of enforcing the object-oriented view, functions only occur as properties of objects. That is, you cannot have a function that doesn't belong to an object. This is the way Java works, for example, and while it is logical it makes many things difficult. For example, in Java you cannot pass a function as a parameter to a method. You can only pass an object that happens to have the function you want to pass as a method.

The fact that in JavaScript functions are just objects that have some executable code associated with them is a very powerful idea, and once you get used to it then it brings a level of freedom that takes time to get used to.

In conclusion:

- JavaScript is a language with lots of bad points, but no more than any language struggling to be both logically consistent and usable.

- If you ignore these minor bad points then what you have is a language that does things in a different, sophisticated and exciting way.

The Development of JavaScript

There is no doubt that Brendan Eich had a clearish view of what he wanted JavaScript to be, but as the language has been improved this view has sometimes been threatened. The constant pressure of programmers wanting JavaScript to be more like Java has been difficult to resist.

For example, in ES2015 a class construct was added to make JavaScript look more like a class-based language. You might think that this would invalidate my description of JavaScript as not a class-based language. However, the class construct in ES2015 is simply a syntactic sugar coating for the familiar prototype inheritance. You can use it to hide from the way JavaScript works and even pretend that it is indeed class-based, but one day reality will bite and you will discover that the syntactic icing is very thin. This doesn't mean that you shouldn't use the class construct – it is a useful shorthand for prototypical inheritance – but it is important you know what it is doing for you.

In short, so far at least, the original JavaScript philosophy is intact and the language has acquired some very nice additional features.

Strict Mode

Strict Mode adds another level of complication to our story. What other language has two different names, a plethora of different versions, and two modes of behavior!? Back in the early days, JavaScript was criticized as a poor imitation of Java, and when ES5 was introduced it added "strict mode".

The idea was that placing the string:

```
'use strict';
```

at the start of a program, or in a function, would cause that program or function to be treated in a different way. Browsers that didn't support strict mode would simply ignore the string as an expression that wasn't assigned to anything.

Strict mode solved some very minor, but apparently very irritating, problems, but it resulted in code that ran differently on browsers that didn't support strict.

It also resulted in yet another way to despise classic JavaScript which was now sometimes known as "sloppy" mode. In practice the value of strict mode is dubious and most of the errors and security problems it fixes are just as easily detected and corrected using a tool such as JSLint.

All of the code in this book works in "sloppy" mode, but where strict mode would change the meaning of the code this is noted.

There is also a stated intention that strict mode is designed to make the introduction of new features to JavaScript easier. As a result, the features that strict mode deprecates are likely candidates for deprecation or modification in future versions of JavaScript. This suggests that they should be avoided if possible, even if you opt for non-strict mode.

The Journey

I hope that reading this book is like a journey where you meet and understand the key ideas of JavaScript. It is assumed that you already program reasonably well in JavaScript, although you might well not know why the things you do actually work, and you might have missed opportunities to use JavaScript in ways that are more in keeping with its approach. Specifically it is assumed you know about if, for and many of the other basic constructs used in a programming language. This is not a complete introduction to JavaScript.

At first I try to give you the simplest approach to the fundamental ideas that motivated JavaScript. Usually this is pure, but it doesn't make programming easy enough and so modern JavaScript contains lots of tweaks to make it easier to use and less verbose. The good news is that so far the additions introduced in ES2015 and ES2016 haven't broken JavaScript. Following on from the explanation of the "pure" idea, you will often find sections, and even chapters, with "advanced" in their title. These describe the extra things you need to know to write good JavaScript. They muddy the waters and make the grand principles harder to see, but you cannot ignore them. As long as you have understood the principles they should be fairly obvious.

Often one of the advanced sections or chapters will require you to know more JavaScript than has been introduced. This forward reference is almost impossible to avoid. The only alternative would be to leave these important idea until all of the basics had been introduced, and risk not having them where they are directly relevant. It is assumed that you either know enough JavaScript to cope with these forward references or are prepared to wait until the complete picture is introduced.

Summary

- JavaScript is a different sort of language. It isn't just another Java clone and learning it will broaden your horizons, even if it doesn't finally please you.

- Most of the popular languages currently in use are object-oriented – including JavaScript. However, most of the other popular object-oriented languages are class-based and strongly-typed. JavaScript isn't class-based and it isn't typed.

- Perhaps the most important feature of JavaScript's approach to programming is the way functions are treated as objects.

- JavaScript is regarded by many as a terrible language because it isn't like Java and it is only for scripting. This is a misunderstanding. JavaScript is related to languages such as Self and Scheme and as such deserves to be taken seriously.

- There have been many revisions of JavaScript and it was finally standardized as ECMAScript because Oracle has "JavaScript" trademarked.

- Classical JavaScript is best regarded as everything before ES5.

- ES5 is currently supported on most browsers and can be considered a reasonable choice as the standard definition of JavaScript.

- ES2015 introduced many big changes and, together with ES2016 and later standards, can be considered modern JavaScript.

- Which version of JavaScript you care to use is a matter of which browsers you want, or need, to support.

Chapter 2

In The Beginning There Was The Object

JavaScript doesn't use classes to create objects. Later you can use a constructor function to create objects, but it is worth understanding how object literals work because these are the workhorses of JavaScript. Unless you are creating a complex library of objects, you really only need singletons created as object literals.

The Object Literal { }

JavaScript is not just an object-oriented language, it is object-based.

That is, in JavaScript the object is the fundamental entity.

In other languages, as well as objects, we have classes and types and these are in many ways more fundamental than objects.

JavaScript doesn't have classes and it doesn't have types in the same way, but it can be made to appear to have both if you insist. It is a language powerful enough to mimic the way other languages work.

In JavaScript everything is an object

(with the exception of null and undefined which we can ignore until later).

When you work with JavaScript you generally start by creating objects that you want to use.

An object is a container that can contain a collection of other objects.

The starting point for all of this is the empty object literal:

{}

The curly brackets mean that this is an object and it can contain other objects within the curly brackets.

Believe it or not this is a valid JavaScript program. If you run it, it creates an empty object which promptly disappears again as the program comes to an end.

So what can you put inside an object?

The simple answer is that an object can store a list of name/object or key/value pairs written as

```
name:object
```

with a separating colon.

These are generally known as the properties of the object.

Multiple properties are entered as a comma separated list.

For example:

```
{prop1:object1,prop2:object2, and so on}
```

At the moment we only know about the empty object so it is difficult to give an example that doesn't look either silly or amazingly abstract depending on your point of view.

But as the idea has been raised, here is a simple non-null object:

```
{object1: {}, object2: {}, object3: {}}
```

This is an object with three properties called object1, object2 and object3. Each of these properties is a null object and hence the whole thing isn't very useful.

However, it is worth pointing out that you can already build objects that are nested and hence tree-like.

For example:

```
{object1: {}, object2: {object3: {} } }
```

or using formatting to make the structure clear:

```
{
   object1: {},
   object2: {
             object3: {}
            }
 }
```

This has object1 and object2 at the "top level" and object3 nested within object2. You can see that this is completely general and makes JavaScript objects tree-like structures.

Later we will discover that the objects that are the values of the properties can be specified as object expressions.

Property Access

Now we come to how to access the properties of an object.

There are two equivalent ways of doing this. The first is to use the dot notation. If you want to specify a particular property of an object you simply write:

```
object.property
```

The second is to use square brackets and write:

```
object[property]
```

Both expressions means the same thing and they give you the object associated with the property. The first looks more like an object property reference and the second is more like an array access. This is perfectly reasonable as the JavaScript object is both an object in the usual sense implemented as an associative array of key value pairs.

Which notation you use depends on a number of different things, but in most cases you should use the dot notation unless you have a good reason not to.

Later on you will discover that the form:

```
object[property]
```

has one advantage that is sometimes vital. The property can be specified by a string which means you can access a property dynamically, i.e. the property accessed can only be determined at runtime.

You can think of this form of property access as being more like accessing an array of values.

The dot form of the property is fully determined at "compile" time and this can allow some optimizations.

If the property is another object and this has properties then you can simply use the same principle again.

For example:

```
object.property1.property2
```

and so on

or:

```
object[property1][property2]
```

and so on.

Referring to a property in this way can be used to change its value.

For example:

```
object.property1={}
```

sets property1 to a new empty object.

You can also create a new property, i.e. add a property to an existing object, by simply assigning something to it.

For example:

```
object.property3={}
```

If the property exists then it is set to a new empty object, but if it doesn't currently exist it is created and initialized to a new empty object.

It is the ability to assign values to properties that don't currently exist that makes JavaScript objects interesting. Objects can be dynamically extended by assignment and this means

all JavaScript objects are dynamic.

The Global Object – Variables?

Before we can get much further with using JavaScript we have to have a way to keep track of the objects we create so that we can use them later in the program.

In most languages this is where variables first appear, but in JavaScript the idea of a variable is more complicated and subtle.

The JavaScript environment provides a standard object called the Global object.

What the Global object is varies according to the execution environment. For JavaScript running in a browser the Global object is a window. However, you can always refer to the Global object, no matter what it actually is, using "this" - but this is mostly unnecessary.

Note: if you know about "this" as used in functions, then it is worth adding that it always refers to the Global object when used outside of a function. Later we will discover that "this" is always the current execution context, and outside of a function it is the Global object which is the top level context.

The role of the Global object is to provide what in other languages would be referred to as global variables. You can create properties on the Global object dynamically simply by assigning to them.

For example:

```
this.myObject={};
```

creates a new Global object property called myObject and sets it to the empty object.

Notice that this is a property on the Global object and not what you would normally refer to as a global variable.

To make the Global object's properties look more like global variables JavaScript has a number of short forms for working with them.

If you simply refer to a property without specifying the object, for example:

```
myObject={};
```

then it is assumed that it is the Global object you are referencing.

To make this look more like a variable declaration you can also write:

```
var myObject;
myObject={};
```

or:

```
var myObject={};
```

but these are just shorthand for:

```
this.myObject={};
```

However, var carries with it the implication that you are declaring a variable and it is treated slightly differently by the system.

As before, remember that within a function "this" has a different meaning.

In JavaScript there are no global variables, only properties of the Global object.

Strict Mode

In strict mode you have to declare a variable i.e. you have to use this or var. Assigning to a variable doesn't create a property on the global object, it throws a runtime exception.

Constructors – Object

You may be familiar with a second and more standard way of creating an empty object:

```
new Object();
```

has the same effect (almost) as using {} i.e. it creates a new empty object.

This is the first example of a constructor – a function that returns an object.

All of JavaScript's built-in objects are created using a constructor and in some cases some other shorthand method is provided. In the case of a basic object you can either call the Object constructor or use the object literal {}.

In principle it should make no difference how an object is created – constructor or some other method – but in practice it often does for reasons of implementation efficiency. In many respects this is one of JavaScript's necessary bad parts.

You can consider the {} syntax more fundamental than the constructor, but the constructor is often more useful and it has a range of facilities that make working with objects easier.

The constructor is the fundamental way to create objects and in this sense it plays the role of a class in other languages.

There is a lot more to say about the constructor.

When you define your own objects you can either use the object literal syntax i.e. {} and then add properties, or you can create your own constructor. The role of the constructor is central in JavaScript object-oriented programming and so it is usually better to create a constructor for any object you want to create. See later – particularly Chapter 9.

Reference Semantics

It is important to realize that variables, i.e. properties of the Global object, store references to objects.

When you create an Object it is tempting to think of the variable that you assign it to as being the name of the Object – it isn't. The object has no name associated with it and the variable is simply a reference – a pointer if you like – to that new Object:

```
var myObject=new Object();
```

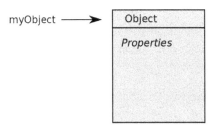

This might seem to be a small matter but it changes the way assignment works.

If you have a reference to an object and store it in another variable, for example:

```
var myObject1=new Object();
var myObject2=myObject1;
```

then myObject2 references the same object as myObject1.

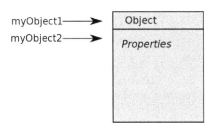

That is, any changes you make using the variable myObject1 will be made to the common Object and those changes will be evident if you access the Object via myObject2 – they reference or point to the same object with the same properties.

That is, after:

```
myObject1.myProperty=newValue;
```

the property access:

```
myObject2.myProperty
```

returns the newValue.

This is quite different to what happens in languages where variables store values. If a variable stores a value then assignment makes a copy of the value.

Even in JavaScript assignment makes a copy – but it makes a copy of the reference to the object – not the object.

Anonymous Objects

In common with many other object-oriented languages, objects in JavaScript do not have fixed immutable names.

In JavaScript objects don't have names, only variables that reference them.

It is important to keep in mind that an object is not the variable that references it. That is, when you write:

```
var myObject=new Object();
```

there is a tendency to think that myObject is the object you just created. It isn't. As already explained, myObject is a variable that holds a reference to the new object which we can only describe as "new object" because it doesn't have a fixed name.

This may seem all very obvious, but not thinking about objects as being something distinct from the variables that just happen to reference them is one of the causes of subtle and hence hard to find errors.

One feature new in ES2015 is const which creates a variable that cannot be changed by reassignment and cannot be redefined. If you write:

```
const myObject=new Object();
```

then you can be reasonably confident that myObject will always reference the new object. In this sense you could consider myObject as the immutable name of the object. However, notice that this doesn't stop other variables from referencing the same object and so providing alternative names.

Another difference between JavaScript and class-based languages is that the class usually has an immutable name. When you create say a Person class this is the only name the class has and it cannot be changed. You might not be able to think of an instance of the class as having a fixed name, but at least it is an instance of a class with a fixed name. This allows you to think of it, say, as an instance of the Person class which does give you some sort of name for the type of object it is. In JavaScript objects can be created without the use of a constructor and you can't rely on even a name for the type of object it is.

The real reason why it is important to keep in mind the fact that objects don't have names is that in JavaScript functions are objects and as such don't have immutable names, only variables that reference them – see Chapter 5.

In other languages when you define a function its name is usually fixed and unchangeable. You might think that when you create a function you assign it a fixed name, but this is just a syntactic convenience to make JavaScript functions look like the named functions of other languages.

In JavaScript all functions are anonymous.

Built-in Objects – String

Now we have the use of the Global Object's properties, we can create objects that we can retain a reference to and use and modify later.

For example:

```
this.myObject={};
this.myObject.newProperty={};
```

or more succinctly:

```
var myObject={};
myObject.newProperty={};
```

The problem is that because the only type of object we know about is the empty object this makes creating anything interesting difficult.

JavaScript has a range of built-in objects which you can just use. All of these built-in objects have constructors but they also have alternative short cut ways of creating instances.

How all this fits together will become clearer as we proceed but for the moment all you need to know is that there is a String object which can represent a string of characters.

You can create a new string object initialized to a given set of characters using the constructor:

```
new String("characters")
```

So:

```
new String("ABCD")
```

is a string object that represents ABCD i.e. its value is ABCD.

There is a subtle point here. Notice that new String("ABCD") is a different object to new String("EFG"). A new object is manufactured each time we use new String.

Notice that if you know how things are actually implemented you will know that strings are not implemented as full objects for reasons of efficiency. However, how you should think about the high level aspects of a language is not the same thing as the messy details of its implementation.

Strings are objects and they have methods and properties.

Using this we can now create an example of a custom object with some properties:

```
var myAddress= { Name:new String("John"),
                 Address:new String("A Town")
               }
```

This is an object with two properties Name and Address. You can guess that the idea is to use this object to represent a name and address. You can also see that we are using two String objects as the objects associated with each property.

You can retrieve the properties in the usual way.

For example:

`myAddress.Name`

and

`myAddress[Name]`

both specify the String object – String("John").

Global Alert, Value & Log

The next problem we have is that we have no way of verifying that any of this actually works – currently you have to take it on trust. We can solve this problem with alert.

When JavaScript runs in a web browser the Global Object, i.e. window, has a number of properties, but the one that is important to us is named alert. It can be used to display the value of any object that you specify.

The value of an object is a fairly obvious representation of the object as readable text.

The idea of the value of an object is something we will have to return to later because it is a more sophisticated idea than you might think and it is very useful.

So for example:

```
window.alert({});
```

displays the text:

```
object:Object
```

which isn't particularly useful but simply means that the object in question is a basic Object and not some other special built-in object. If you try the same thing with a String object then you will see the text that it represents. For example:

```
window.alert(new String("ABCD"));
```

displays the text ABCD.

There are two simplifications we can make to the code.

The first is that as window is the global object we can write:

```
this.alert(new String("ABCD"));
```

or just:

```
alert(new String("ABCD"));
```

The second is that the String object is so important that you can just write "ABCD" to create a String object with the value "ABCD".

So our display instruction can be reduced to:

```
alert("ABCD");
```

Which is probably the form you already know how to use.

Such syntactic simplifications are useful but they tend to hide the principles of operation of JavaScript.

If you know how strings are represented you will know that "ABCD" does differ from new String("ABCD"). The literal string "ABCD" is represented as a primitive string for efficiency reasons, but JavaScript will pretend that it is an object any time it has to – see the section Primitive Problems.

As an alternative to alert most browsers and IDEs provide a global console object complete with a log method which will display any string in the console window. The problem that most beginners have is finding the console window. To do this you generally have to open the debugging facilities either in the browser or in the IDE you are using.

Both alert and console have their advantages but neither are perfect as debugging or exploratory tools.

Built-In Objects – Number

As you would guess, just as there is a String object there is a Number object. If you try:

```
alert(Number(3));
```

you will see the number 3 displayed. You have created a Number object with the value 3.

JavaScript doesn't distinguish between different types of number – so no ints and floats. You can use integers, whole numbers, or decimal numbers such as 1.234 as values for Number objects.

This has implications that we have to look at later but for now you can just accept the simplification of not having to worry about different representations of numeric values.

Don't underestimate the value of this simplification to a beginner.

When you start to explain to a non-programmer that there are two types of number, floats and ints, you can see their eyes glaze over and a deep mistrust of such silliness creeps into their soul. Later is the time to worry about integer v floating point operations, not right at the start of learning and not in everyday programming. The language should take care of the messy things in life and if you don't agree with this there is always assembler waiting for your return.

What beginners find difficult is what a language should try to remove.

Representations Are Not An Issue

If you think that explaining the difference between float and int to a beginner is difficult then you aren't going to want to go into how 1 is not the same as "1".

It is very hard for the seasoned programmer comfortable with the distinction between 1 and "1" to see that these two things are the expression of the same idea. One is a Number object and the other is a String object.

The problem is that we focus too much on the representation of the data. We know that the underlying binary representation of numeric 1 is different from the representation of string "1" and this means we don't treat them in the same way.

But we have just swept the representation problem for floats and ints under the rug, why not strings and numerics?

Representation is not something that should trouble a high level language programmer unless it matters in some tricky technical way.

This is a principle that JavaScript tries to apply, but it is very difficult and yes it doesn't always make the right choices.

In theory, JavaScript would not make a fuss about any form of representation of data. JavaScript does treat the Number 1 and the String "1" as being very similar and in many cases they can be used interchangeably. This too can cause problems, but again it is an initial simplification and another important one for the beginner. Again, the representation of data is not something that a language should force you to consider every time you write a simple instruction.

The point of a high level language is to take away as many of the low level concerns as possible, and this is something that a lot of modern languages have forgotten or sacrificed in the name of strong data typing.

In JavaScript if something looks like a number then you can use it as a number even if it is surrounded by quotes.

For example, both:

```
var twopi=2*3.14159;
alert(twopi);
```

and:

```
twopi=2*"3.14159";
alert(twopi);
```

display the same numeric result.

This is shocking to many an experienced programmer – you cannot multiply a string by numeric 2 – but it is natural from the point of view of a beginner.

The principle is simple – **treat data that a human would consider the same in the same way irrespective of its representation which is a matter for the compiler not the programmer.**

The only problem is that this is a very difficult thing to do and to do properly would need something approaching AI. JavaScript does perform automatic conversion between fundamental data types – coercion – and this is the source of much criticism. However, it makes getting started so much easier and you can always perform the conversion manually using the many data conversion functions.

The same sort of approach applies to comparing two objects. Again JavaScript takes the approach that two objects that look alike should be treated alike. In JavaScript, but not in many other language 1=="1" is true. However you can also use the strict equality operator which gives 1==="1" as false. The question of when two objects are equal all depends on what you mean by equality. The == operator compares object values and the === operator compares objects.

A Number Really Is An Object

Because you can write things like:

```
var myValue=10;
```

programmers often over look the fact that in JavaScript a number is an object.

You can dynamically create properties on Number objects as you can on any object and this can be something of a shock if you haven't encountered it before.

For example:

```
var myObject=new Number(3);
myObject.myProperty="My Age";
alert(myObject.myProperty);
```

will display "My Age".

In JavaScript simple numeric values can have properties.

Of course, you don't have to write new Number() to create a Number object, you can simply write its value, as in:

```
var myObject=3;
```

Now here we hit a snag – primitives.

The Primitive Problem

The idea that everything in JavaScript is an object is an ideal – and one not quite lived up to.

For efficiency reasons, when you make use of a Number literal like 3, JavaScript doesn't create a Number object. It stores the 3 as a primitive data value.

The same is true of String literals like "ABC" and of boolean, null and undefined – all of which will be described later. What matters at the moment is that idea that there are types of data that are not stored as objects for efficiency reasons.

That is:

```
var myObject=3;
```

actually creates a primitive value and not an object.

However, JavaScript does its best to pretend that myObject is a Number object.

If you try to make use of a property of the Number object like:

```
myObject.toString()
```

then JavaScript will oblige and convert the primitive value to a Number object and call the method.

This automatic conversion is called boxing, and the problem is that for efficiency JavaScript immediately unboxes a primitive value. This doesn't matter when you are trying to make use of built-in properties, but if you try to add a property it will be immediately lost on unboxing.

If you want to make use of custom properties on numbers, you have to explicitly box the value using the Number constructor as in the examples given earlier.

In practice this doesn't have any real impact on what you want to write because you don't often want or need to add custom properties to the built-in objects.

To be clear:

- ◆ JavaScript's primitive data types behave like objects that you cannot add properties to – that is, they cannot be customized.
- ◆ If you create the data type using, say, new Number, then you get a complete object that you can use and customize.

There is also an interesting extra problem in that if you try to use a property on a numeric literal using the "dot" notation, it doesn't work. The reason is that JavaScript interprets the dot as a decimal point.

So you have to write not:

```
3.toString();
```

but:

```
(3).toString();
```

or:

```
3["toString"];
```

These exceptions are a shame because they spoil the deep principles.

Strict Mode

In strict mode you cannot create a property on a primitive data type, and if you try it throws a runtime exception. In non-strict mode you can do it but because of boxing and unboxing it has no effect.

Expressions and Immutability

One of the main tools of any programming language is the expression.

An expression takes data and combines it to produces new data.

For example, an arithmetic expression takes numbers and combines them to make new numbers. The ways in which the data can be combined takes the form of different operators. So arithmetic expressions have the addition operator and multiplication and so on.

For example:

```
2+3*4
```

is an expression that combines 2, 3 and 4 and produces a new value of 14.

When you think of expressions in JavaScript you are encouraged to think of the operators as working with objects to create new objects.

For example:

```
2+3*4
```

combines three Number objects with values 2, 3 and 4 and creates a new Number object with the value 14.

In this sense you can imagine that the String and the Numeric objects are immutable – they don't change their values, they are simply used within expressions to create new objects with different values.

The fact that an expression always creates a new object is a natural idea that explains all sort of minor apparently odd behavior in JavaScript.

For example if you try:

```
var myObject=new Number(3);
myObject.myProperty="My Age";
var myObject2=myObject;
alert(myObject2);
alert(myObject2.myProperty);
```

You will find that myObject2 has a myProperty and its value is "My Age". This is because myObject2 refers to the same Number object, myObject.

However, if you make the small change to the code and add one to myObject as in:

```
var myObject=new Number(3);
myObject.myProperty="My Age";
var one=new Number(1);
var myObject2=myObject+one;
alert(myObject2);
alert(myObject2.myProperty);
```

You will find that myObject2 has a value of 4 ,but it doesn't have a myProperty i.e. it is undefined.

The reason is that the arithmetic expression generates a new Number object that doesn't have a myProperty unless you go to the trouble of recreating it.

That is, expressions that combine objects always create a new object.

Of course there is the complication of primitive data but in the main you can ignore it. The simple reason is that a primitive data value behaves as if it has only the default properties of the object, and so when you combine them in an expression you get something that has just the default properties. Once again it looks as if expressions take in objects and spit out a new object – even with primitive values.

In short, you can always think of expressions as working with objects and creating a new object as the result.

There is much more about this idea in Chapter 4.

Summary

- Everything in JavaScript is an object.

- The basic object is the empty object literal {}.

- Objects can also be created using the Object constructor function.

- Object have properties, which are name:value pairs.

- The value of a property is always an object and hence an object can represent a general tree structure by nesting objects.

- The Global Object provides properties that can be used as if they were global variables.

- All Objects are anonymous in JavaScript.

- Variables reference objects.

- The const modifier can be used to create an immutable reference to an object.

- The Global Object also provides some properties that are functions and these, like alert, can be used as always available functions.

- The built-in objects String and Number allow data to be stored in objects as values.

- The built-in objects are always created using a constructor function.

- Primitive data values behave as if they only have the default properties of the object. This is done for reasons of efficiency.

- Objects have values which cannot be changed.

- Expressions create new objects with values derived from the objects involved in the expression.

Chapter 3

Real World Objects

It would be nice if all there was to say about JavaScript objects was the ideas introduced in Chapter 2. In fact, there are various facilities that have been introduced to make objects more usable. While these don't change the basic philosophy of JavaScript, they can cloud the issue when you first start learning the language. In this chapter we look at some features that make real world objects easier to use.

Advanced Objects – Expression Value and Key

Later on you will discover that there is a general rule that anywhere you can use an object you can use an object expression.

What this means in this case is that the object that is the value of a property can be produced by an expression.

For example:

```
{object1:1+2}
```

creates a property called object1 with the value numeric object 3.

In ES2015 you can also use variables to create properties. In this case the name of the variable is the name of the property and its value is its value.

For example:

```
var object1=1+2;
var object2={};
{object1,object2};
```

creates an object with properties object1:3 and object2:{}.

Also in ES2015 you can use an expression to set both the name and the value of a property. For example:

```
{["myproperty"+n]:n}
```

assuming n is set to 1, this creates an object with the property myproperty1:1.

Advanced Property Access

Since ES2015 you have been able to define computed properties using get and set. If you are familiar with other object-oriented languages you might already be familiar with the idea of getters and setters. Instead of a direct access to a property a get function is automatically called on access and a set function on assignment.

For example:

```
var myObject={
    value:0,
    get myValue() {return this.value;},
    set myValue(v) {this.value=v;}
    };

myObject.myValue=10;
alert(myObject.myValue);
```

In this case the object has a property called myValue in addition to value. Notice that the name of the property is myValue and not getmyValue or setmyValue. When you assign to myValue the set function is automatically called with the value assigned. In this case the call sets the "normal" property value to 10. When myValue is accessed as in the alert function, a call to the get function automatically occurs to supply the value. Notice that in this case value is a publicly accessible property – you can create a private property but this relies on using a constructor.

Also notice the use of this.value to refer to the value property of the object. This is the call context and will be discussed in more detail in Chapter 8.

The main use of get and set is often said to be to compute a property from other properties. For example, area derived from a length and width property. In most cases, however, the main use of set is to verify that the property value is valid. For example if you have a property which is a percentage then you can write:

```
var myObject={
    value:0,
    get myValue() {return this.value;},
    set myValue(v) {
                    if(v<0) return;
                    if(v>100) return;
                    this.value=v;
                  }
    };
```

The main use of get is to convert an internal representation of a value into something more useful.

For example, you might have a library that works with days of the week coded as 0 to 6 but prefer to expose this as the more usual 1 to 7:

```
var myObject={day:0,
    get myValue() {return this.day+1;},
    set myValue(v) {
                    if(v<1) return;
                    if(v>7) return;
                    this.day=v-1;
                }
    };
```

This is a fairly trivial example but the general principle is that:

◆ set is used to check for legality and to pre-process data

◆ get is used to convert data representation

Advanced Property Creation

As we have discovered, you can create a new property by simply using it. However, you cannot create a getter or a setter property in this way as you also have to define the get and set functions. To allow for more complex properties to be added dynamically and to allow for more control over how properties behave there is the defineProperty method of the Object constructor.

You can use it to add a property to myObject using:

```
Object.defineProperty(myObject,'myProperty',descriptor);
```

The optional descriptor is an object of key value pairs that defines the property.

You can use any of the following keys:

```
configurable — default true
```

set to true if the property is dynamic and its descriptor may be changed and the property deleted. You can still change the value but any attempt to change other characteristics of the property results in a runtime error.

```
Enumerable — default false
```

set to true if the property is to be included in an enumeration of properties using for..in say.

```
value — default undefined
```

The value of the property.

```
Writable — default false
```

set to true if value can change. If the property isn't writable then attempts to change its value fail but no error is thrown.

```
get default undefined
```

a getter function for the property

```
set default undefined
```

a setter function for the property.

If you specify get and set you cannot specify writable or value, they are mutually exclusive.

So for example:

```
Object.defineProperty(myObject,'myProperty',{value:0,
                                            writable: true,
                                            enumerable: true,
                                            configurable: true
                                            });
```

is equivalent to:

```
myObject.myProperty=0;
```

i.e. the usual way of creating a property. Notice that the defaults do not give you the usual way of creating a property.

You can use defineProperty to control how properties behave but note that it was only defined in ES5.1 and only fully defined in ES2015.

If the property already exists then any key value pairs you include are used to modify it.

There is also a defineProperties method which allows you to define multiple properties:

```
Object(myObject,properties)
```

where properties is an object which consists of name descriptor pairs. For example:

```
Object.defineProperty(myObject,{myProperty1:{value:0,
                                             writable: true,
                                             enumerable: true,
                                             configurable: true
                                             },

                                myProperty2:{value:0,
                                             writable: true,
                                             enumerable: true,
                                             configurable: true
                                             }
                                });
```

creates myProperty1 and myProperty2 with the descriptors as given.

Object Creation

We already have two ways of creating an object as a literal {} or using the Object constructor. There was a need to find a more flexible way to specify the object that was being created and ES5.1 introduced the object factory method create.

Object.create works in much the same way as the constructor itself but you can specify another object to be used as the Prototype. Prototypes are described in Chapter 8 and you will find more on Object.create there.

So:

```
Object.create(null);
```

returns an object with no prototype – this is the purest object you can create as it has no properties at all.

You can also specify an object to create properties. This object consists of property names with values that are property descriptors as introduced in the previous section.

For example:

```
var myObject= Object.create(null,{myProperty:{
                                    value:0,
                                    writable: true,
                                    enumerable: true,
                                    configurable: true
                                  }
                  });
```

Creates an object with a single property, myProperty, with the characteristics as given.

You can see that Object.create is a much more precise way of creating an object with just the characteristics you need, but note that it isn't supported by older browsers. If you can assume ES5 or ES2015 then it is the preferred way of creating an object but preferable within a constructor – see later.

Object Mutability

Three new methods were introduced in ES5.1 and fully specified in ES2015 – freeze, seal and preventExtension. These bring a degree of object immutability to JavaScript. If you can make use of them, they are supported from IE9 and later, then they make using objects much more reliable.

The highest level of immutability is provided by freeze which stops any modification to the object. That is, you cannot add or remove properties. You cannot modify the configuration of existing properties including the property value. Finally you cannot change the object's prototype – see Chapter 10.

Following:

```
Object.freeze(obj);
```

all you can do is access any readable properties or call methods.

The main problem with freeze is that it is only a shallow immutability. Any properties that reference objects are frozen in the sense that you cannot assign a new object to them, but the objects themselves can be changed.

That is, objects that are properties of a frozen object are not themselves frozen.

If you want a deep frozen object then you have to make sure that any properties that are objects are also frozen – and so on.

One level down from frozen is sealed. A sealed object has a fixed set of read/write properties. That is, sealing an object stops the addition or deletion of its existing properties. The non-configurable state is also set and while the prototype chain is unaffected you cannot change the prototype of the object.

A sealed object has a fixed set of own properties.

Finally we have the preventExtensions method which simply blocks any attempt to add own properties to the object. You can still delete own properties and you can add properties to the object in the prototype chain, however, you cannot change the prototype chain.

You cannot undo the effects of freeze, seal or preventExtensions.

The three approaches to immutability have in common a vagueness about what is supposed to happen if you try and change something that isn't changeable. In most cases if you try and change an immutable property then the operation will just fail silently unless you have set strict mode when most likely an exception is thrown.

The JavaScript approach to mutability is useful but far from perfect. In particular it doesn't distinguish between methods and data. Methods are described in Chapter 8 but essentially they are properties that are functions – see Chapter 5. In many cases you want to allow modifications to data properties but not to function properties. That is, you want to allow the data to be changed but not the code. The problem is that freeze, seal or preventExtensions treat all properties the same. That is freeze means you can't modify data or methods and seal and preventExtensions mean you can modify data and methods.

You can of course set properties to read only for methods and then use seal to stop them from being modified.

For example:
```
obj.display=function(){alert("Hello");};
Object.defineProperty(obj,'display',{ writable: false,
                                       configurable: false
                                     });
```
makes display an immutable property and any attempt to change the function will cause a runtime exception. If you set all of an object's properties to the appropriate writable status and then seal the object you have an object that is only mutable in the way that you want it to be.

Summary

- A general principle is that anywhere you can use an object you can use an object expression.

- The value of a property can be an object expression.

- In ES2015 the name of a property can be taken from a variable and its value is the variable's current value.

- You can create getters and setters for any property.

- In general a set is used to check for legality and to pre-process the data and a get is used to convert data representations.

- The Object constructor has a set of methods that allow you to work with objects in more sophisticated ways.

- The defineProperty method can be used to control how properties behave.

- You can use defineProperties to add a set of properties to an object.

- The create method allows you to specify the prototype object.

- The methods freeze, seal and preventExtension can be used to impose various levels of immutability on objects.

Chapter 4

The Object Expression

As in most programming languages the expression is an important part of JavaScript, but it isn't quite the same. This is where the idea that JavaScript has some weird type conversions arises. But in reality JavaScript isn't too fussy about type and it doesn't really do conversions.

Expressions form a mini-computer language inside most computer languages. The good news is that the way that they work is more or less the same in all languages. The symbols used for the operators change, the priorities change, and occasionally there are some additional operators.

An expression is essentially a generalization of the way arithmetic works. For standard arithmetic we only have four operators +, -, * and / standing in for the usual symbols for add, subtract, multiply and divide. These are all binary operators and take a value on the left and one on the right, the operands, and combine the two values to give a new value.

In this chapter we use some simple properties of JavaScript functions which are introduced in the next chapter.

Object Expressions

In programming languages, and in JavaScript in particular, there are generally a lot more operators than four, but they work in the same way taking two values and producing a new value.

In JavaScript you can think of a binary operator as taking two objects and producing a new object.

In many cases this distinction isn't important, but thinking in this way does make it easier to understand what is going on.

For example, take a careful look at:

```
var a=new Number(2);
a.myProperty="Hello World";
alert(a.myProperty);
a=a+1;
alert(a);
alert(a.myProperty);
```

What do you expect to see?

First we create a Number object with value 2 and a custom property myProperty. When you display the property it shows "Hello World" as you would expect. Next we add one to a and display its value, which is 3 as you would expect, but now the property is "undefined".

All we did was add one to a, surely this can't have modified the property?

It not only modified the property, it created a new object. When you add two Number objects together the result is a new Number object.

You can make this clearer by writing:

```
a=a+new Number(1);
```

and you will see that now the + operator takes the object referenced by a and the Number object we have created and adds their values together. As the result is a new object, it isn't surprising that it doesn't have the custom property you set on the first Number object.

JavaScript expressions combine objects and produce a final object.

This isn't the way things are implemented in the JavaScript engine but this is more a matter of implementation detail than any deep philosophical approach.

Of course primitive values are operated on in their unwrapped non-object state in reality but for the sake of a good logical story we can ignore this as it makes no practical difference to how things behave.

All Objects Have Value

In principle any operator in JavaScript can take two objects, any two objects, and produce a new Number, String or Boolean object.

In JavaScript there are three important types of operator – those that produce Number objects, those that produce String objects and those that produce Boolean objects.

It turns out that the way Boolean operators work is different for various reasons.

For now let's just concentrate on Number and String operators.

The only String operator is concatenation which is represented by the same symbol as addition, +.

The main Number operators are +,-,* and /. Other Number operators work in similar ways so it is reasonable just to consider these four.

You can use any object in an expression, not just Number and String. For example:

```
myObject1+myObject2;
```

is perfectly valid irrespective of what the objects are.

How can general objects be included in expressions?

The answer to this question is that every JavaScript object has a value as returned by the valueOf method.

Methods are discussed in detail in Chapter 8 but for now you can treat a method as a property of an object that is used like a function.

The valueOf method is intended to return an object that is somehow regarded as the "value" of the object.

Usually the value is a Number or a String but in fact it can be any object you care to return.

In practice, however, if it is going to be used with the standard operators it has to be a primitive object – i.e. a Number or a String.

When you use an object in an expression its valueOf method is automatically called to find a primitive value to use in the expression.

For example:

```
var myObject={};
myObject.valueOf=function(){return 1;};
var a=new Number(2);
a=a+myObject;
alert(a);
```

You can see that the myObject's valueOf function returns 1.

You can also see that in:

```
a+myObject;
```

myObject behaves as if it had a value of 1, as you would expect.

In other words:

```
a+myObject;
```

is equivalent to:

```
a.valueOf()+myObject.valueOf()
```

Notice that when you write:

```
a+1;
```

you can think of this too as:

```
a.valueOf()+1.valueOf();
```

All operands in a string or numeric expression have an implied valueOf call to provide the primitive value used in the evaluation of the expression.

The Concatenation Operator

This simple picture is made more confusing by the way + is used to represent addition and String concatenation.

How does JavaScript tell when you mean add and when you mean concatenate?

The rule is very simple.

If either operand in:

```
Object1 + Object2
```

returns a String from its valueOf method then the operator is String concatenation.

For example:

```
var myObject1={};
myObject1.valueOf=function(){return "MyString1";};
var myObject2={};
myObject2.valueOf=function(){return "MyString2"};

a = myObject1 + myObject2;
```

In this case both valueOf methods return String objects and so the operator is concatenation and the result is:

```
MyString1MyString2
```

The same rule applies to the += operator which is concatenation if either a or b is a String in a+=b.

However, notice that a+=b is the same as a=a+(b) which is not always the same as a=a+b because b will be evaluated first.

Now we come to the interesting question of what happens if only one of the two objects involved in the expression has a String value?

In this case by the rule we have just introduced the + is String concatenation but only one of the objects is a String.

The answer to this question is slightly more complicated than you might think – but very reasonable once you understand it.

But first a simple quiz.

Expression Quiz

To make sure you have all of this worked out, see if you can answer the following questions:

1. What is   1 + 2 + "3" + 4 + 5

2. What is   1 + "2" * 3

3. What is   "4" + 1 + "2" * 3

4. What is the final value of a a="1";
                                a = a + 2 + 2;

5. What is the final value of a   a = "1";
                              a += 2 + 2;

Try to work them out without typing in the code, then see if you are right by running the code. Even if you are right, see below for the full explanations.

Answers

1. **"3345"**

    Reason: All the + operators have the same priority and are hence evaluated from left to right. The first operator is 1+2 and so the answer is Number 3. The second operator is now 3+"3" and as one of the operands is a String the first 3 is converted to a String and the result is "33". The third operator is now "33"+4 and by the same reasoning this is concatenation and the result is "334". The final operator is "334"+4 and again this is concatenation and the result is "3344".

2. **7**

    Reason: * has a higher priority than + so the first operator is "2"*3 and after "2".valueOf() the result is 6. The second operator is now 1+6 so the result is Number 7.

3. **"416"**

    Reason: * has the higher priority so the first operator is "2"*3 and after "2".valueOf() the result is 6. But now the + operators have equal priority and the expression to evaluate is "4"+1+6. The first operator is "4"+1 which evaluates to "41". The final operator is "41"+6 which evaluates to "416".

4. **"122"**

    Reason: The first operation is concatenation and hence so is the second.

5. **"14"**

    Reason: Despite this looking like the previous example, the expression on the right is evaluated first and then the a+ operation is performed. That is, it is equivalent to a=a+(2+2); or "1"+4.

Every Object Has a String Value

Just as the valueOf method gives every object a value, the toString method does the same sort of thing for strings.

- ◆ Every object has a toString method that can be used to supply a String representation of the object.
- ◆ You can define your own toString method or you can accept the use of the default.
- ◆ You can provide a toString method to a custom object as in the case of the valueOf method.

For example:

```
var myObject={};
myObject.valueOf=function(){return 1;};
myObject.toString=function(){return "myString";};
```

Now we have a custom object which has a value and a String representation.

As in the case of valueOf, you don't have to return a String object as the result of a toString method, but not to do so would be misleading in the extreme.

So when is toString used in an expression?

There are two ways that toString can be invoked during the evaluation of an expression.

The first is to get a primitive value for the object.

Put simply, if the expression evaluator fails to get a primitive object from valueOf it will try toString to get one.

That is, it first uses the valueOf method. If this returns a primitive value then it stops. If this returns a general object the evaluator next tries the toString method to see if this can provide a primitive value. If this works the value is used in the expression; if it doesn't then you get a runtime error:

```
Cannot convert object to primitive value
```

To see this in action try:

```
var myObject1={};
myObject1.valueOf=function(){return {};};
myObject1.toString=function(){return {};};
a=1+myObject1;
```

Notice that in this case both methods return an empty object, which isn't a primitive value.

Notice that toString can return a Number object and this will work:

```
myObject1.valueOf=function(){return {};};
myObject1.toString=function(){return 1;};
a=1+myObject1;
```

This doesn't throw a runtime error and it results in 2 stored in a.

The evaluator doesn't care about what type of primitive object it gets from valueOf or toString – as long as it is a primitive object.

The second way the toString method can be called is if the primitive value obtained earlier is the wrong sort of primitive.

For example, consider concatenation. You might think that if one of the operands in the expression was a String:

```
a=myObject1+"1";
```

then the toString method would be called to convert the other object to a String.

This isn't what happens.

What happens is the same two steps – first valueOf is called and if it doesn't provide a primitive value toString is called.

At this point we assume we have a primitive value, pv, ready to be used in the expression.

If the expression turns out to be concatenation, because of the other operand being a String, then the toString method is called on the primitive value, i.e. pv.toString() is used in the expression. The original object's toString method isn't used.

This is because the object's value is more important than its String representation.

For example:

```
var myObject1={};
myObject1.valueOf=function(){return 1;};
myObject1.toString=function(){return "One";};
```

followed by:

```
"1"+myObject1;
```

is "11" because valueOf returns 1 which is a primitive value and then 1.toString() is called to give "1" which is used in the concatenation. Object1's toString method doesn't get used.

Also notice that it doesn't matter which of the two methods returns the primitive value.

The same sort of thing happens if your custom object returns a String primitive value when the expression needs a Number. In this case the primitive value's valueOf is called in an attempt to obtain a Number primitive.

If this doesn't work the result of the expression is NaN – Not A Number.

Recap

Putting all this together:

1) JavaScript expressions are evaluated in order of precedence and then left-to-right (in most cases) for equal precedence operators.

2) All objects involved in an expression are first converted to a primitive value using valueOf.

3) If any valueOf method doesn't return a primitive value, i.e. a String or a Number, then its toString method is used to get a primitive value, i.e. a String or a Number.

4) If neither valueOf or toString returns a primitive value then there is a runtime error.

5) If the primitive value obtained in step 2 or 3 is of the wrong type for the operator, then toString or valueOf is called on the primitive type to convert it.

Built-In Objects and Type Conversion

Built-in objects like String have a predefined valueOf method that returns sensible values for the object.

What is a sensible value for a String?

The obvious answer is a String.

What is the sensible value for a Number?

The obvious answer is a Number.

So far so good.

In both cases valueOf returns the same primitive type as the original object. In a sense a Number and a String are their own object values.

What happens if a Number is involved in an expression that requires a String?

The answer is that its toString method is called.

What happens if a Number is involved in an expression that requires a string?

In this case the internal toNumber method is called. You can't make use of the toNumber method but it is automatically called to convert a String to a Number when required.

Consider, for example:

```
var a=new Number(2);
var num=new String("123");
a=a*num;
alert(a);
```

In this case when the String object is used in the expression a*num then its default valueOf method is called automatically and it returns a primitive string. Next, internally, the toNumber function is called to convert the value of this string to a number. If the string cannot be converted then the result is NaN – Not a Number.

Type Conversion?

By analogy with other languages, most programmers think of this as type conversion. That is, a Number is converted to a String or vice-versa. It is usually referred to as type coercion because in most cases neither you, nor the data, have any choice in the matter.

However, there is a better way to think of what is happening.

JavaScript doesn't have types in the same way that other languages do. It is as type-free as it is possible to get.

In other languages variables have an assigned type and they can only reference an object of a compatible type.

In JavaScript variables don't have a type and they can reference any object.

In this sense JavaScript doesn't support type.

It does recognize the primitive values – Number, String and Boolean and their associated wrapper objects. These are the only things that work with the standard operators and hence any object that is involved in an expression has to have a primitive value associated with it. When an object is used in an expression it provides its associated primitive value. If that value is the wrong type of primitive value then the system will convert it if it is possible.

You can think of this as type conversion but it really is a very degraded use of the term when you compare it to the complex type hierarchies that are found in class-based languages.

It is better regarded as representation conversion. If you have a String which stores "123" and you want to add 1 to it then you need to change the representation of the number from "123" to 123 and then add 1.

Some Strings are valid representations of numbers and all numbers have a valid String representation.

Objects With Custom Values

Once you are happy with the idea that general objects can have values associated with them you can start to make use of this.

For example:

```
var digit={
            value:"",
            valueOf:function(){
                        if(this.value=="One") return 1;
                        if(this.value=="Two") return 2;

                              ...
                        return NaN;
                  }
            };
```

This defines a simple object that represents the digits 1, 2 and so on as words. The valueOf method converts this representation into a Number representation in a very simple way.

Now you can write things like:

```
digit.value="One";
var a=1;
a=a+digit;
alert(a);
```

and you will see that digit has worked correctly within an arithmetic expression.

What you can't do is provide a toString method that will work correctly in all cases. For example:

```
var digit={
            value:"",
            valueOf:function(){
                        if(this.value=="One") return 1;
                        if(this.value=="Two") return 2;

                              ...
                        return NaN;
                  },
            toString:function(){
                        return this.value;
                  }
            };
```

In this case the toString will work when you try things like alert(digit) but in an expression the valueOf will be called first and this will provide a Number. If a String is required the system will call the Number's toString method not digit's toString.

Comparison Operators

Once you have the idea that first valueOf is called and then toString if necessary then JavaScript expressions become much easier and more logical.

The comparison operators can be used with Number or String but they come in two forms – type-converting and strict.

The type-converting operators fit in with JavaScript's philosophy even if beginners are often warned against using them.

The rule for the way a type converting comparison operator works is exactly the same as for the addition/concatenation operator.

If you use a comparison operator and one of the operands is a string, then the toString method is called on the value returned by valueOf.

So for example if myObject is:

```
var myObject={};
myObject.valueOf=function(){return 1;};
```

then:

```
1==myObject;
```

is true because there are no String objects involved and valueOf returns Number 1.

Also:

```
"1"==myObject;
```

is true because there is a String object involved, valueOf returns Number 1 and 1.toString() is "1".

The strict comparison operator === doesn't ever call valueOf and never performs a type conversion by calling toString, it simply compares the two objects for type and value. The only things it considers equal are equal primitive values of the same type or two references to the same object.

In this case both:

```
1===myObject;
```

and:

```
"1"===myObject;
```

return false because despite the fact that both objects have the same values they are different types. The 1 is a Number object, the "1" is a String object and myObject is just an instance of Object.

This is usually where the discussion of equality and strict equality stops and the point is made that strict equality is much safer and logical. However, even strict equality can be more complex than the above example because of the possibility that its operands are expressions in their own right.

For example:

```
1 === myObject;
```

is false because the operands are different objects but:

```
1 === +myObject;
```

is true because now the right-hand side is an expression and in its evaluation myObject's valueOf method is called and this returns a Number 1 object which is regarded as the same as the Number 1 object on the left.

However, notice that:

```
"1" === +myObject;
```

is false because the toString conversion isn't called for the valueOf result from myObject, but if you write:

```
+"1" === +myObject;
```

the result is true because +"1" calls the String's valueOf method before the comparison.

Note that putting a + in front of anything is an easy way to convert anything into an expression without modifying its value.

The idea that the strict equality operator takes type into account is only true if its operands are not expressions.

There is one final complication that you need to be aware of.

JavaScript needs some way of testing to see if two variables reference the same object. Rather than introduce a new reference equality operator the standard operators, both == and === test for reference equality when both operands are references to objects rather than expression or primitive values.

What this means is that if you define two objects with valueOf methods:

```
var myObject1={};
myObject1.valueOf=function(){return 1;};
var myObject2={};
myObject2.valueOf=function(){return 1;};
```

then the tests:

```
myObject1==1
myObject2==1
```

return true as the valueOf method is called. If you were to use === the result would be false because the objects are not Number objects and valueOf is not called.

If you now try:

```
myObject1==myObject2
```

or:

```
myObject1===myObject2
```

the result is false because the two variables do not reference the same object.

If you want to compare two objects using their valueOf method you have to explicitly make one or both an expression.

For example:

```
myObject1 == +myObject2
```

or:

```
+myObject1 === +myObject2
```

both return true because they need to evaluate the expression and hence valueOf is called and both objects return Number 1.

However, notice that the strict equality operator will not call toString to make a type conversion but == will.

The issue of which is best == or === is more complicated and subtle than most accounts explain and they both have dangers that are best avoided by understanding rather than just using one or the other.

The other operators work in the same sort of way but with the usual complication over what less than and greater than mean for a String.

Recap

To summarize:

1. There are two equality (and inequality) operators == and the strict equality operator ===.

2. If the operands are both object references op1==op2 and op1===op2 work in the same way and return true only if the two operands reference the same object.

3. In all other cases op1==op2 calls valueOf by default and toString if needed before the test, and op1===op2 doesn't and just performs the comparison between primitive types.

4. You can always force valueOf to be called by adding a unary plus + in front of the operand.
   Thus +op1===+op2 is almost the same as op1==+op2, but it doesn't automatically call toString if type conversion is required.

Functions in Expressions

As well as objects you can also include function evaluations within an expression.

For example:

```
var a=2*myFunction();
```

in this case the function can return a general object and the valueOf and toString methods are used as described earlier to obtain a primitive value of the correct sort.

For example if myFunction returns a custom object then its valueOf method is called to obtain a primitive value etc..

What is interesting is that as a Function object is an Object, see the next chapter, it too can define valueOf and toString methods.

So for example:

```
var myFunction=function(){return 1;};
myFunction.valueOf=function(){return 2};
```

defines a function which returns 1 as its result but also has a valueOf property that returns 2 as its value.

Now you can write:

```
var a=2*myFunction();
```

and the result is 2 or:

```
var a=2*myFunction;
```

and the result is 4.

The difference is that in the first the function invocation operator () is used to evaluate i.e. execute the function which results in 1 being returned. In the second case the function is treated as an object within the expression and is valueOf method is called which returns 2.

You could also put a function evaluation in the valueOf method so that the function can be called with or without () and parameters.

```
myFunction.valueOf=function(){return this()};
```

Now writing myFunction() returns the same as writing myFunction.

The Object Expression Principle

Now that we have all of the fine detail of how object expressions work, it is time to state the key principle of using expressions in JavaScript – the Object Expression Principle:

Anywhere you can use an object you can use an expression

At this point you might be thinking that this is not particularly useful as expressions evaluate to primitive values – Number, String or Boolean. However, as you can use a function in an expression, a single function evaluation is also an expression and in this case the return value can be any object.

This one simple idea makes it possible to do a lot of things that would otherwise be very difficult.

For example when you are defining an object literal you can write:

```
var myObject1={myProperty:myObject2};
```

which sets myProperty to be a reference to myObject2.

However, if you write:

```
var myObject1={myProperty: +myObject2};
```

then myProperty will be set to whatever myObject2.valueOf returns.

And finally:

```
var myObject1={myProperty: myObject2()};
```

sets myProperty to whatever the function body of myObject2 returns.

Of course this last one assumes that myObject2 is a Function object. If it isn't you generate a "not a function" runtime exception.

The ability to use an object expression anywhere an object can be used might seem obvious or a small thing, but in practice it turns out to be a very powerful idea that makes a lot of interesting things possible.

Often the use is so commonplace that you might not even have noticed that this is exactly what is going on.

Summary

- JavaScript expressions combine objects to produce a final object.

- As JavaScript's operators all work with primitive types the final object is always a primitive type.

- All objects have a value which is determined by evaluating the valueOf method.

- In general, an object's value has to be a primitive type if it is to be used in an expression.

- The only ambiguous operator in JavaScript is the + operator which is either addition or concatenation. Which it is depends on its operands. If either operand returns a String then it is concatenation and the other operands also have to provide String values.

- Every object also has a String value which is provided by the toString method.

- If the valueOf method fails to provide a primitive type during the evaluation of an expression the toString method is called to see if it provides a primitive type. If neither provides a primitive type then a runtime error occurs.

- If the valueOf method returns a Number and the expression needs a string the toString method of the Number object is called and not the original object's toString method.

- If valueOf returns a String and a Number is required then the String's valueOf is used.

- The == comparison operator also uses valueOf to obtain a primitive value to compare, but the === operator does not.

- The === operator tests for equality of primitive values or equality of object reference.

- Both operators test for equality of reference if the expressions being compared are simple references.

- Anywhere you can use an object you can use an expression.

Chapter 5

The Function Object

In this chapter we meet the most important object of all – the Function object. What really matters is that you don't think that it is just a function.

In JavaScript there are no functions – only Function objects.

As we keep reiterating JavaScript is an object-oriented language, but not in the sense that you might know from languages such as C++, Java or C#, say. JavaScript is different and in the style of Smalltalk and similar dynamic object-oriented languages where everything is an object.

Other object-oriented languages break the "everything is an object" rule, most crucially when it comes to functions, but JavaScript doesn't.

The mainstream object-oriented languages give in to the very natural pressure to make code special.

You want to write a program – so you want to get on and write some code but where does that code live?

In non-object based languages there is only the code. You start to write a list of statements, and that is all there is to the program.

So when you first start writing programs you tend to think that the code is the most important thing, but later you learn about objects and you are told that code is just a property of an object, i.e. the object's methods.

That is, the language has objects and objects have properties which are usually other objects, and they also have methods which are blocks of executable code.

That is, the answer to the question of where does the code live, in the case of an object-based language, is that code exists as methods which aren't objects but a special type of property that an object can have.

Objects are the main entity in the program and can be assigned and passed around. The code is always bound to some object or other and so you can't do things like pass code as a parameter because it isn't an object. This makes tasks such as event handling and callbacks difficult.

So in most object based languages there are objects and there are methods – which are executable properties.

Constructing Function Objects

JavaScript takes a different approach to the problem of code by introducing the idea of the Function object.

A Function object is created in the way any built-in object is, via a suitable constructor, and used in the way all objects can be used.

To create a new Function object you use:

```
new Function();
```

For example:

```
var myFunction= new Function();
```

The use of new is optional.

Once created you can add properties to the new object in the usual way:

```
myFunction.myProperty="hello function";
```

The point that is being made is that the Function object is "just an object like any other".

So what additional characteristics does the Function object have that makes it useful?

The simple answer is that a Function object can accept some code as part of its creation.

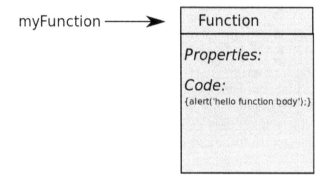

Of course we now need to know what statements JavaScript supports that we can use in the code of a Function object. For the moment only a very simple set of statements are used.

When you create a Function object you can specify a list of statements that form the function's "body".

For example:

```
var myFunction= new Function("alert('hello function body');");
```

This creates a Function object with a body that consists of the single statement:

```
alert('hello function body');
```

So a Function object has some code stored within it.

This code is immutable after the Function object has been created – you can't modify it. If you want to change the code you have to create a new Function object.

The code may be immutable but it is specified as a String and this means that it can be the result of a String expression which computes the code at runtime. It is this possibility that makes it impossible to optimize this way of specifying a Function.

You also need to take careful note that the code that constitutes the body isn't executed when the Function object is created. The body can be thought of as a sort of default property of the Function object – i.e. the Function object simply stores the code for you. In fact there is a [[Call]] property that only Function objects have, but it is an internal property and not accessible within JavaScript code.

All you can do with the function body is execute the code it by using the function invocation operator ().

For example:

```
myFunction()
```

causes the list of statements that make up the Function object's body to be executed. In this case it simply causes an alert box to appear with the message.

Notice that:

```
myFunction;
```

without the function invocation operator, is a variable that references the Function object and:

```
myFunction();
```

i.e. with the function invocation operator, evaluates the body of the Function object that myFunction references.

It is also important to realize that Function objects are anonymous just like all JavaScript objects. That is, they do not have names built-in to their definition. They simply have variables that reference them. This is very different from most other languages and notice that this also applies to function expressions and function statements – see the later section.

In JavaScript, functions do not have names just references.

Function Variables

The code in the function body can declare local variables and these are not properties of any object. Local variables only come into existence when the function is executed and they are destroyed i.e. removed from memory when the function finishes. They are also private to the function and cannot be accessed by any other code. They can be accessed by functions that are defined within the function concerned and this is something we need to consider in more detail later.

To create a local variable you have to use the var keyword:

```
var myLocalVariable=0;
```

This creates a local variable which only exists while the function is executing. The unexpected detail is that due to hoisting, see later, local variables exist for the entire lifetime of the function irrespective of where they are declared.

If you don't use the var keyword then the variable is interpreted as a property of the global object. For example:

```
myLocalVariable=0;
```

is the same as:

```
this.myLocalVariable=0;
```

As explained earlier, properties of the global object behave like global variables in other languages.

One side effect of using properties rather than global variables is that when you write:

```
myVariable=0;
```

then if the property doesn't exist it will be created. What this means in practice is that forgetting to use var in a function adds properties to the global object that you probably never intended to add. Most IDEs and smart editors will warn you if you don't use var in a function. In practice it is better to always use this to access or create a property or var to create a variable.

Strict Mode

In strict mode you have to use var in a variable declaration. If you don't then a runtime exception occurs. Also in strict mode the global object 'this' inside a function is undefined. This means a function cannot easily create a global variable or access the global object. Notice that this doesn't stop a function from using a global variable, only creating a new one.

Return and Parameters

You might well be thinking if the invocation operator evaluates the function it should return a result and this is the case. You can use the statement:

```
return result;
```

to specify what the function evaluates to.

If you don't specify a return result the function body returns undefined.

For example:

```
var myFunction= new Function("var ans=1+2;return ans;");
```

has the function body:

```
var ans=1+2;
return ans;
```

Now if you try:

```
alert(myFunction());
```

you will see 3 displayed as this is the result of the function.

The value of the function can be any object not just a Number object (actually a primitive value) as in the example.

The final part of the Function object we need to examine is the use of parameters.

In other languages you have to specify what parameters are to be passed to a function but in JavaScript you don't. When you call a Function you can simply supply as many arguments as you like as a list of comma separated objects. The list is used to create an array like object called arguments that is available to the code of the Function.

For example:

```
var myFunction=
    new Function("var ans=arguments[0]+arguments[1];return ans");
```

and now you can call the function using:

```
alert(myFunction(1,2));
```

and you will see 3 displayed. The arguments 1 and 2 are automatically converted into the properties of the arguments object as arguments[0] and arguments[1].

Notice that this means that when you define a function you can call it with as many arguments of any type you care to use.

This mechanism is the basic way that JavaScript deals with function parameters but, of course, it is nothing like the way other languages allow you to specify parameters. To make coding easier and more familiar JavaScript allows you to specify a parameter list of variables when you define a function.

For example:

```
var myFunction= new Function("a","b","var ans=a+b;return ans");
```

The values that you specify when you call the function are still used to create the arguments object but they are also used to create the local variables a and b with a=arguments[0] and b=arguments[1] and hence the function will return the sum of a and b no matter what they are set to when the function is evaluated.

For example:

```
alert(myFunction(1,2));
```

sets a to reference 1 and b to reference 2 and then evaluates the body.

Notice that function parameters can be any object and not just the Number objects used in the example. You can also think of what is passed as being a reference to an object, even it it happens to be a primitive value, in all cases.

You can also use as many parameters in a function definition as you care to define and use as many as you care to when you execute the function. For each parameter you give a value to there is a variable of the same name with that value as part of the function's code. Any missing parameters are undefined and it is up to your code to deal with this.

Also notice that this implies that there is **no JavaScript form of function overloading because functions don't have fixed signatures**.

In fact parameters in JavaScript are a little more subtle than this and we will have to come back to them later after we have found some more convenient ways of creating Function objects – see Chapter 7.

Other Ways Of Creating Function Objects

You could just use the Function object approach to creating JavaScript code but it isn't exactly convenient to have to enclose all code in quotes or form a String object.

This said, there are times when converting a String object containing code into an executable Function object is useful, but these tend to be considered advanced techniques.

JavaScript before ES2015 provides two other ways to define a Function object and they both look more like function definitions in other languages – the Function expression and the Function statement.

The purpose of the Function expression is to give you a way to define a function without using a String to store the code. This is more secure and it allows for optimizations. A Function expression also looks a lot like a lambda expression in other languages.

ES2015 also introduced "arrow" functions as a forth way of defining a Function object. Arrow functions look even more like lambda expressions in other languages but this isn't their real purpose as JavaScript has long had adequate support for lambdas in the form of the Function expression. Arrow functions are mostly about writing functions using a more condensed syntax and they solve a long standing problem with the way methods are implemented using this.

The purpose of a Function statement is to make JavaScript Functions look more like functions in other objects. A Function statement obscures the fact that you are creating an object and it appears to give the function a fixed name. It also allows a style of programming based on a "top-down" approach to work because of the application of hoisting – see later.

Notice that even though these look different they also create a Function object just like the constructor although with some differences.

Lets' start with the Function expression.

The Function Expression

This is just a shortcut to creating a Function object and doesn't really introduce anything new but you can now write:

```
function(parameters){statements};
```

Notice that the function body is now specified as statements enclosed in curly brackets and it is specified as part of the program text not as a String.

This means that it cannot change at runtime and so the JavaScript engine is able to make optimizations that cannot be made when the code is specified as a possibly dynamic String. That is, with a function expression the function's code is known and fixed at "compile time" and hence more easily optimized.

Enclosing the code in curly brackets {} is also the notation used to create compound statements in JavaScript – that is, any list of statements enclosed in curly brackets is regarded as a single statement.

For example the previous Function object can be written:

```
var myFunction=function(a,b){var ans=a+b; return ans;};
```

or by including line-breaks to produce a more usual formatting:

```
var myFunction= function(a,b){
                var ans=a+b;
                return ans;
              };
```

This has the advantage that this looks more like a function definition in a non-object-oriented language. In particular it also looks a lot more like a lambda expression which you will find in most modern languages.

It is important to keep in mind that while this looks like a simple function declaration as you would find in other languages it isn't.

A function expression creates a Function object exactly like the Function constructor does.

Also notice that the variable assigned to becomes a reference to the function object as with the constructor.

Also notice that again just as when you use the constructor the Function object is anonymous. All you can do is to set a variable to reference it but those variables can be set to reference something else at any time.

The Arrow Function ES2015

The arrow function is mostly a condensed syntax for the function expression. You can use it to define a function as simply as:

```
(param1,parm2…, parmN)=> {statements};
```

For example:

```
(a,b)=>{
        var ans=a+b;
        return ans;
    };
```

This returns a Function object which can be used in the normal way.

For example you can store a reference to the arrow function in a variable:

```
var myFunction=(a,b)=>{
                    var ans=a+b;
                    return ans;
                };
```

and you can call the function in the usual way:

```
myFunction(1,2);
```

There are some syntactic shortcuts you can use, but this is more or less all there is to an arrow function – with one exception. Arrow functions do not have a this of their own, they inherit whatever value for this is in use at the time of their declaration.

This makes them unsuitable for use as method definitions but much better for passing to other Functions as parameters.

Apart from this everything that is true of a function expression is also true of an arrow function.

Now we need to look at the Function statement.

The Function Statement

In an ideal world the account of the Function object would come to an end at this point – you have enough to write any program you care to but not in a style most programmers would recognize.

Most languages introduce functions using a statement not an expression. The idea of assigning a reference to a function to a variable is something that many languages have only recently added under the name "lambda functions" or "lambda expressions",

JavaScript has this other way of defining a function – the Function statement. Instead of writing an assignment you simply write:

```
function functionname(parameters){
    function body
}
```

This results in a Function object with the specified parameters and function body being created – as before.

What appears to be new is the *functionname*. This is handled in a slightly different way by the JavaScript engine but it behaves much like a standard variable and you can assign it a new value. Think of the function statement as declaring the *functionname* variable.

Function names are in fact treated in special ways; in particular the function name is "hoisted". It is as if the function declaration was positioned at the top of the program or of the function it is declared in so that the function can be used before it has been defined. Hoisting is described in more detail in the next section but the reason that JavaScript implements such a seemingly odd action is that this is how other languages tend to work with respect to functions. In a more traditional language you can write a main program that uses functions that are defined later in the text of the program. JavaScript achieves the same result by using hoisting.

Notice that Function objects created using the constructor or an expression are not hoisted and have to be declared before their first use.

Function names can be assigned to and generally treated like variables but they are also used by debuggers to report information on functions and how you are using them. Apart from hoisting, a statement function works in the same way as a function expression.

If you really want to you can confuse the issue by assigning a function name in a function expression. That is:

```
var myFunction1=function myFunction2(){};
```

where both myFunction1 and myFunction2 are variables that reference the same function object, but myFunction2 is local to the Function object – see later.

Hoisting

Hoisting is usually introduced much later in an account of how JavaScript works, but it is a fundamental idea and it is about the distinction between declaration and initialization. It is most often encountered in connection with function statements, but it actually applies to all declarations.

There is a subtle difference between:

```
this.property=value;
```

and:

```
var property=value;
```

JavaScript implements hoisting of declarations to make it possible for you to use Global Properties before they have been fully declared.

The rule is that every:

```
var property=value;
```

statement is first split into:

```
var property;
property=value;
```

and then the var part of the instruction is moved to the very top of the containing part of program.

In other words, the declaration is moved to the top but the initialization is left in place. This means that the property exists from the moment the program runs but it isn't initialized until execution reaches the place in the program you intended it to be initialized.

For example if you try:

```
console.log(myvar1);
console.log(myvar2);

var myvar1 = "test";
this.myvar2 = "test";
```

You will find that you see "undefined" displayed in the console log for myvar1 because it has be hoisted, i.e. declared but not initialized, whereas the attempt to display myvar2 throws a runtime exception of variable not defined as it hasn't been hoisted and hence declared.

In most cases you can forget hoisting and just write:

```
var property=value;
```

where the initialization makes sense.

Variables that are declared within a function are hoisted to the top of the function's code.

For example:

```
function myFunction(){
  console.log(myvar1);
  var myvar1=0;
}
```

is transformed by hoisting into:

```
function myFunction(){
  var myvar1;
  console.log(myvar1);
  myvar1=0;
}
```

and the result is that the variable is undefined at the point you try to display its value.

Hoisting of variables within functions usually goes unnoticed until a local variable shadows a global variable.

For example:

```
var myvar1=10;
function myFunction(){
  console.log(myvar1);
  var myvar1=0;
}
```

In this case you would expect the myvar used in the console.log statement to be the global variable, as the local variable of the same name hasn't be declared yet.

This isn't what happens, however, because hoisting converts the function into:

```
var myvar1=10;
function myFunction(){
  var myvar1;
  console.log(myvar1);
  myvar1=0;
}
```

and the result displayed is "undefined".

As already mentioned, hoisting also applies to a function statement.

For example:

```
function myFunction(a,b){return a+b};
myFunction(1,2);
```

works perfectly because myFunction is defined before you use it, but in fact due to hoisting this consideration doesn't matter. Moreover:

```
myFunction(1,2);
function myFunction(a,b){return a+b};
```

also works perfectly as the function declaration is hoisted to the top of the section of code. Notice that functions that use the Function expression, or the constructor, are not hoisted. That is:

```
myFunction(1,2);
var myFunction = function(a,b){return a+b};
```

gives a runtime error.

Function Objects Are Anonymous

As has already been explained, all objects in JavaScript are nameless, or anonymous if you like, and Function objects are no different. However, in most other languages functions are tied tightly to a single name and this makes JavaScript different. This name usually indicates what the function does. For example you might define the max function which finds and returns the maximum of two numeric values, and in many languages this would be the immutable name of the function.

In JavaScript, however, there are no immutable object names and in particular no immutable Function names.

There are small exceptions to this rule in that if you give a name to an expression function then this is created as a local variable – see later.

In JavaScript you can create a max function in any of three ways.

Using a constructor:

```
var max = Function("a", "b", "if(a>b)return a;return b;");
```

Using a function expression:

```
var max = function (a, b) {
            if (a > b)
                 return a;
            return b;
      };
```

Using a function statement:

```
function max(a, b) {
          if (a > b)
              return a;
          return b;
        };
```

In each case you can call the function in the usual way:

```
alert(max(3,4));
```

but you can also make things slightly more difficult by creating a new reference to the function:

```
var min=max;
alert(min(3,4));
```

Now you are calling the same function but using the "name" min. Many programmers are happy that the first two function definitions work like this but are surprised that the function statement doesn't confer a fixed name on the function. Notice that the variable max can be assigned a new value so removing even the possibility of calling the function using the "name" max. For example:

```
max=0;
max(2,3);
```

Results in a "not a function" error.

Of course it goes without saying that the same is true of arrow functions as they are just shorthand expression functions.

Although function names assigned using Function statements are often regarded as the assigned names of the Function object, they are just as much variable references to the object as in the case of the constructor or the Function expression. They tend not to be modified but only because this is the way programmers think about them.

It is worth mentioning that ES2015 introduced the Function.name property which records the name given to the function when it is first created. If you try:

```
alert(max.name);
```

you will see anonymous for the constructor and max for the Function expression and Function statement. The name property cannot be changed by assignment but you can use defineProperty to change it. As the name property is a String you can't use it to directly call the function and hence it isn't as useful as you might expect. At best you can use it to check the name that the function was assigned when it was created.

Constructor v Expression v Statement

Apart from hoisting and some matters of optimization, there isn't much difference between the three different ways of creating a Function object. However, you should use function expression/arrow or function statements in preference to the constructor because the JavaScript engine can optimize these better.

Although the function name supplied as part of a function statement looks like an immutable name, as it would be in most other languages, all three ways of creating functions create anonymous Function objects.

There is one other important difference between function expressions and statements compared to Function objects created using the constructor. The constructor always creates an object that is in the global scope. That is, it cannot be used to create functions that are local to other functions, whereas function expression and statements can create local functions. More of this is in the next chapter where we look in detail at scope, lifetime and closure.

Function Properties

The final fundamental characteristic of a Function object which makes JavaScript functions different is that they can have properties as well as code.

You can create properties of a Function object just like any other object. As long as you are fully aware that a function in JavaScript is an object, then this is not a surprise, but this is one of the most overlooked features of JavaScript. In practice you rarely see functions with properties.

For example:

```
var myFunction= function(a,b){
                var ans=a+b;
                return ans;
            };
myFunction.myConstant=3.14159;
alert(myFunction.myConstant);
```

There is nothing new here. The variable myFunction references a Function object and we can dynamically create a new property, myConstant. Later we can access the property's value in the usual way.

What is new is the possibility of referencing a property of the function within the code of the function.

For example:

```
var myFunction= function(a,b){
                var ans=a+b;
                return ans*myFunction.myConstant;
            };
```

Now at this point you might be worried by the idea of using myFunction.myConstant before the function has been fully declared. Of course, you are not actually using myFunction.myConstant before the function has been fully declared because the property is only accessed when the function is evaluated.

That is, the code for the function is stored in the Function object and as long as the code makes sense at the time it executed everything works:

```
myFunction.myConstant=3.14159;
alert(myFunction(1,0));
```

At the point the function is called myFunction and myFunction.myConstant both exist and are fully defined.

There is just one problem with this approach. What if myFunction is redefined? In this case myFunction.myConstant will reference a property on some other object when the function is executed.

This is another example of the Function object being anonymous and the variables that reference it are mutable.

For now the most common solution to the problem is to use a Function statement and pretend that the function name you assign isn't something that can be changed – it can, but few make use of this in practice.

For example:

```
function myFunction(a,b){
            var ans=a+b;
            return ans*myFunction.myConstant;
        };
myFunction.myConstant=3.14159;
alert(myFunction(1,0));
```

works perfectly and few programmers would think to redefine myFunction. Of course if myFunction is reused then things don't work:

```
var myFunction2=myFunction;
myFunction=0;
alert(myFunction2(1,0));
```

In this case the call using myFunction2 works in that it references the same Function object as myFunction did, but the function no longer works because it uses myFunction to reference itself.

The problem is that there is no elementary way that a Function object can make a "self" reference. You can't use this because this is the call context and in this case it is set to window – the global object.

Function Self Reference – callee

The arguments object is discussed in more detail in Chapter 7, but it has a callee property which is a reference to the currently executing function. This makes it very easy to write code that references properties of the Function object without having to worry what the function is called.

For example, if we write the previous function as:

```
function myFunction(a,b){
        var ans=a+b;
        return ans*arguments.callee.myConstant;
    };
myFunction.myConstant=3.14159;
alert(myFunction(1,0));
```

then the function will work no matter what variable is used to access it.

If you want to write functions that work with their own properties then it is a good idea to create a shortcut reference to arguments.callee:

```
function myFunction(a,b){
        var self=arguments.callee;
        var ans=a+b;
        return ans*self.myConstant;
    };
```

Strict Mode

The one problem with using the callee property is that in strict mode this is not allowed and any attempt to use callee generates a runtime error. There are also moves to remove callee from a future version of JavaScript. Fortunately there is a better, although slightly more complicated, way of achieving the same result.

Function Self Reference – Named Function Expressions

In an effort to provide a name for functions, ES2015 introduced named expressions. A named expression looks a lot like a statement function, but one that you assign to a variable.

For example:

```
var myFunction1=function myFunction(a,b){
                var ans=a+b;
                return ans*myFunction.myConstant;
            };
myFunction1.myConstant=3.14159;
alert(myFunction1(1,0));
```

The variable myFunction1 works in the usual way, but myFunction is a local variable. That is, myFunction can only be accessed within the function and it cannot be changed by external code. It can be redefined within the function, but as long as you don't do this it can be used within the function's code as a self reference.

Function Self Reference – Advanced

It is possible to add a self reference to a Function object without using callee or a named function expression, but in its most convenient form it requires a constructor or factory function and the action of closure to create a private variable. All of these topics are covered in later chapters, but the need to include a self reference within a Function object is so useful that it is worth presenting the technique here.

The basic idea is to use a factory function which creates the Function object you want. There are two advantages of using a factory function. The first is that the Function object can be set up exactly as you want it before it is consumed and the second is that you can use closure to create a private variable.

The only downside is that you have to think up a name for the factory function as well as a typical name for the function it produces:

```
var myFuncFactory = function () {
```

You can use a Function statement if you want to. Next we create the Function object storing a reference to it in a local variable:

```
  var self = function () {
            return self.myValue;
          };
```

In this case the function simply returns the value of a property of the Function object. If we want to the object factory can also create the property and initialize it:

```
self.myValue=0;
```

You can see that we can use self to reference the Function object whenever we need to.

Finally the object factory has to return the Function object:

```
 return self;
};
```

Putting all this together gives:

```
var myFuncFactory = function () {
                    var self = function () {
                                return self.myValue;
                            };
                    self.myValue=0;
                    return self;
                };
```

You can see the general principles:

- ◆ use a factory function to return the Function object
- ◆ set a local variable self to reference that Function object
- ◆ use self within the function definition to reference any properties of the object
- ◆ use self to create properties.

To use the factory function all you do is:

```
var myFunction=myFuncFactory();
```

Now when you call the function:

```
alert(myFunction());
```

the execution of the code has no dependency on what you call the variable that references the function.

Summary

- In JavaScript functions are objects created by the Function constructor.

- The Function constructor takes a String as the function's code body and this can be dynamically determined at runtime. This makes optimizations difficult to apply.

- You can evaluate a function using the invocation operator ().

- Function bodies can contain local variables which only exist while the function is executing.

- Functions do not have parameters specified in their declaration and can be called with as many arguments as are required.

- As parameters are not typed or fixed in number, there is no function overloading in JavaScript.

- Functions can return an object of any type as a result.

- As well as the Function constructor, you can also create Function objects using a function expression, arrow function or function statement.

- Function statements are subject to hoisting where the definition is moved to the start of the function's scope.

- Functions, no matter how created, are anonymous and only have variables that reference them.

- As functions are objects, they can have properties and the code associated with the function can reference these properties using either callee, named function expressions, or a via a private variable created by closure.

Chapter 6

Functions – Scope, Lifetime and Closure

In this chapter we look at some of the more advanced ideas involved in JavaScript functions leading up to the very useful, but often misunderstood, idea of closure. Most of the complexities arise from the simple fact that once you have a Function object you can execute its code and this code can in turn create variables and most importantly additional Function objects.

Scope and the Execution Context

Now we come to the much talked about idea of scope and how JavaScript implements it.

Scope refers to which variables you can access at any point in code.

Before we go on it is worth considering where the variables that are declared in the function body live. They are clearly not properties of the Function object. In fact, they don't even exist except when the function body is being evaluated.

That is, all of the variables in the function body are created when the function body is evaluated and destroyed again when it finishes.

What happens is that when a function body is evaluated, an Execution Context EC is created which stores all of the variables that are accessible from the code. You can think of the EC as being an object with properties that are the variables that are in scope – although you can't directly access the EC and it is an implementation detail.

If you remember from Chapter 2 that variables you create outside of a function are in fact properties of the global object, you can see that the global object plays the role of an EC object for code that lives outside of a function. You can also think of the code that you write outside of a function, i.e. at the global level, as being the function body of the global object – but this is perhaps an abstraction too far.

That is, when the function body is evaluated the variables that are in scope form the execution context.

In the case of JavaScript the scope rules are very simple but only if you realize that you are working with Function objects and not functions.

In JavaScript variables are said to have function scope.

This means that when a function body is evaluated the variables that are created are only accessible within that function.

That is, all variables declared within a function are essentially "local" variables and override any variables already declared elsewhere.

Notice that all local variables only exist while the function is executing – they are not properties of the object. That is, local variables are created anew each time the function is executed.

Things are a tiny bit more complicated than this because JavaScript, like most other languages, actually allows nested function scope in that any function can make use of variables defined in any function that contains it.

We need to consider what "contain" means.

In JavaScript objects can "contain" other objects as properties.

In the same way a Function object can contain other objects as properties, but in addition a Function object can create additional Function objects when its function body is evaluated.

For example:

```
var myFunction= function(a,b){
              var ans=a+b;
              var myInnerF=function(){
                          alert(ans);
                          };
              return ans;
            };
```

Notice that we have a new Function myInnerF created when myFunction is evaluated.

In this case we say that myInnerF is "nested" within, or contained within myFunction.

This doesn't mean that myInnerF is somehow a property of the myFunction Function object. What it means is that myInnerF is created when myFunction is evaluated. It is the declaration of the new function that is nested within myFunction. There is no sense in which the Function object created is in any way contained or nested within the Function object referenced by myFunction.

The new Function object is exactly like any other Function object and it is referenced by a local variable myInnerF of the function body.

Also notice that a new Function object is created each time myFunction is evaluated. This is often a cause of inefficiencies because it is easy to forget that functions are really Function objects. When myFunction finishes evaluating, the local variable, myInnerF, is destroyed and eventually so is the object it references when it is garbage collected by the JavaScript engine.

At this point it looks as if declaring a function inside of another function simply changes how long the inner function lives but there is more to it.

The "nested" scope means that myInnerF can not only access its own local variables, it can also access any variables that are local to the containing function i.e. myFunction in this case. As you can see in this example it makes use of ans which is local to myFunction.

The nested idea applies when multiple functions are nested inside each other. Each inner function has access to its own local variables and the variables of all of the functions that contain its declaration.

So in this case both myFunction and myInnerF also have access to the variables defined within the Global object. In this sense all functions are nested within the Global object.

This notion of nested scope when functions are objects is a very subtle idea.

The reason is when you look at the function body of a Function object there is a tendency to think that it is being executed as you read it.

This isn't the case.

If you look at our example, first the outer Function object is created and its function body is stored.

When you execute the outer function body, at some later time the inner Function object is created but its code isn't executed until it is invoked perhaps at a much later time. In this particular example the inner function isn't evaluated but it can be and this has some strange consequences because of nested scope.

Lifetimes

The fact that a function is actually a Function object makes it possible for the function to exist in its own right independently and irrespective of how and when its function body is evaluated. The local variables of a function only exist when it is being executed but its properties exist at all times.

This is another strange idea if you are familiar with functions in other languages.

Function objects exist complete with any properties you may have defined even when they are not being evaluated.

If you are going to understand some of the more subtle ways that JavaScript works you have to be 100% clear about the lifetime of a function object.

When a Function object is created as part of some code, the Function object is created and it exists within the whole program just like any other object.

As already explained, JavaScript provides automatic garbage collection which removes any object that has no references to it. So an object, any object including a Function object, exists as long as there is at least one reference to it.

Now consider the implication for the nested function that we have looked at in the previous section:

```
var myFunction= function(a,b){
              var ans=a+b;
              var myInnerF=function(){
                          alert(ans);
                      };
              return ans;
          };
```

As already explained, the inner Function object referenced by myInnerF doesn't exist until the outer function is evaluated. That is when you write:

```
myFunction(1,2);
```

the inner Function object is created when the system reaches the line

```
var myInner= etc.
```

This Function object exists from that point on till the end of the outer function i.e. until after the return ans; statement.

At this point the variable myInner goes out of scope and no longer exists. With no variables referencing the inner Function object it is soon garbage collected and so in effect as soon as the outer function ends the inner function no longer exists – not quite true but close enough for most purposes.

So this is a bit restrictive in that the only code that can ever evaluate the inner function has to be part of the outer function body. The reason is that this is the only place that the myInnerF variable is in scope.

Now consider what happens if the inner function has a variable that references it that isn't local to the outer function.

In this case the inner function can actually live longer than the outer function because it still has a variable that references it and hence it won't be garbage collected.

That is, not only can the inner function object exist after the outer function has completed, it can exist when the outer function object has been destroyed. Their lifetimes are quite independent of one another.

This is yet another strange idea but perfectly natural if you think in terms of Function objects.

Function objects stay alive and potentially active as long as there is a variable that references them.

Sounds complicated – but you get used to it.

For example:

```
var myFunction= function(a,b){
 var ans=a+b;
 this.myInnerF=function(){
   alert(ans);
  };
 return ans;
};
```

Now the inner function is referenced by a Global variable – recall that this references the Global object – to be more precise it references the execution context but more of this later.

Note: if you want to use this in strict mode make sure you declare myInnerF as a global variable outside of the function.

Now we can call the outer function:

```
myFunction(1,2);
```

and when the function returns the global variable, myInner references the Function object created within the outer function.

As there is still a reference to the inner Function object it isn't garbage collected and so still exists after the outer function has finished evaluating.

What this means is that you can still evaluate the inner function long after the function body that created it has finished executing and perhaps even long after the outer Function object that declares its function body has been destroyed.

For example:

```
this.myInnerF();
```

will display the Alert box and you will see the value in ans at the time the inner function was created, even though the outer function has finished running some time ago and all its local variables no longer exist – recall local variables only exist while the function is being evaluated.

You can see that by allowing functions to have nested scope we have to allow the inner function to use local variables belonging to the outer function even after those local variables have been destroyed because the outer function has completed.

OK this is all fine, but how can the inner function have access to a variable – ans – that doesn't exist any more?

This is what closures are all about.

Closures

As the lifetime of a Function object only depends on what variables reference it, just like any other object, it can exist well after any outer function that created it.

By the rules of nested scope the inner function has access to the variables in the outer function when it is executed.

The only problem with this is that the local variables of the outer function only exist while it is executing and this means that in principle the inner function can only access them if it is executed as part of the outer function's code i.e. only during the time that the outer function is executing.

The idea of a closure simply extends this access to all times.

In other words nested scope persists beyond the evaluation of the outer function and even beyond the lifetime of the outer function and all its local variables.

If this wasn't the case then having inner Functions with their own lifetimes and nested scope would be very complicated.

The rule would have to be something like - an inner function has access to the local variables of an outer function but only while the function is being evaluated. If you evaluated the inner function at some later time then you would simply get an error message because variables that you could access at one time are no longer accessible.

This would mean that you would get a different result according to when and where you evaluated the inner function.

Using a closure means that the inner function always has access to the same variables no matter when or where it is evaluated.

To be more precise, when a Function object is created all of the variables which are in scope, including those of any outer functions, are stored in an execution context – this what was explained right at the start.

What is new is that the execution context stays with the Function object even when the variables no longer exist because the function body which created them has finished running or the Function object that it belongs to has been garbage collected.

Put another way- a Function's execution context remains its execution context as long as it exists.

There is an important exception to this rule.

Functions created using the Function constructor are always created in the global scope and they do not create closures using the current execution context.

As another example consider:

```
var myFunction= function(){
                var message="Hello Closure";
                this.myInnerF=function(){
                                alert(message);
                                message="Goodbye Closure";
                                };
                };
```

The first line of myFunction creates a local variable message which is added to the execution context and set to "Hello Closure". Next an inner function is defined and a reference to it is stored in the Global variable myInnerF. The function body shows an alert box with what is stored in message and then it changes the message. This demonstrates that you can access and change what is stored in a variable that is provided courtesy of a closure.

With this definition you can now do the following. First you can execute myFunction;

```
myFunction();
```

This evaluates the body of the function and hence results in the creation of the Function object with the function body:

```
 this.myInnerF=function(){
                alert(message);
                message="Goodbye Closure";
            };
```

Notice once again that the inner function is not evaluated, this just sets up the Function object and its function body.

Now you can set the variable myFunction to null which results in there being no more references to the outer Function object and so it is garbage collected – that is its Function object no longer exists and the message variable should no longer exist.

Even so you can still evaluate the inner Function object. The first time:

```
this.myInnerF();
```

you will see:

```
"Hello Closure"
```

and the second time you evaluate it:

```
"Goodbye Closure"
```

It seems the message variable is alive and well, even if the Function object and its function body that is it local to are most certainly not.

When you first encounter the idea of a closure it seems complicated and arbitrary – why do thing in this way?

Why invent the idea of a closure?

Once you follow the fact that functions are just objects, and a Function object can live longer than the Function object that created it, and there is nested scope you begin to see why closures are natural.

They are a natural consequence of letting an inner function access the variables of all of the outer functions that contain it.

To make this work a Function object has to capture all of the variables that are in scope when it is created and their values when the outer functions have completed.

This last point is subtle.

See if you can work out what happens if we make a small change to the last example and if you can also work out why it happens:

```
var myFunction= function(){
            this.myInnerF=function(){
                        alert(message);
                        message="Goodbye Closure";
                    };
            var message="Hello Closure";
        };
```

The only change is that now message is defined after the inner function. You might reason that message isn't in scope but that would be to forget hoisting.

If you recall, all variable declarations are moved by the compiler to the top of the function they occur in.

So the code is equivalent to:

```
var myFunction= function(){
            var message;
            this.myInnerF=function(){
                        alert(message);
                        message="Goodbye Closure";
                    };
            message="Hello Closure";
        };
```

This means that the variable is in scope, and even though it isn't assigned until the end of the outer function, i.e. after the definition of the inner function, its final value is part of the closure. The reason is that the execution context stores the variables and their changing values until the outer function stops.

That is, the execution context captures the final value of the outer functions local variables.

So the new version still displays the two messages as before.

Execution Contexts Are Shared

There are some slightly subtle points that we have to cover.

For example, what happens when there is more than one inner function and hence more than one closure?

The key idea is that there is only ever one execution context for a given Function invocation and any Functions created within that execution context share it.

That is, each time a Function is executed an **execution context** comes into existence consisting of all of the variables that are in scope. Any Functions created while the original Function is executing have that single execution context as their closure – i.e. it is shared.

Notice, however, that each time a Function is executed a new execution context is created along with new inner Function objects.

Consider the following code:

```
var myFunction=function(){
            var myVar=1;
            this.myF1=function(){
                     alert(myVar);
                };
        myVar=2;
        this.myF2=function(){
                 alert(myVar);
                };
        myVar=3;
    };
```

You can see that myFunction creates two inner functions, myF1 and myF2, and the execution context has a single local variable in it i.e. myVar. The question is, what value does myVar have in myF1 and myF2?

```
myFunction();
myF1();
myF2();
```

You should have no problem in predicting that you see the value 3 twice. Both functions share the same execution context and the same myVar which has the value it was assigned when myFunction concludes.

Now consider the slightly more complicated case:

```
var myFunction=function(){
                var myVar=1;
                this.myF1=function(){
                            alert(myVar);
                            myVar=2;
                };
                this.myF2=function(){
                            alert(myVar);
                            myVar=3;
                };

        };
```

This is almost the same, but now myFunction sets myVar to 1 which is its value in the execution context when either of myF1 or myF2 is called. So if you use:

```
myFunction();
myF1();
myF2();
```

you will see 1 displayed, and then myF1 sets myVar to 2 which is what you see displayed by myF2.

That is, myF1 and myF2 share the same execution context and hence they have the variable myVar in common.

Variables that functions have access to due to closure are often referred to as "private" variables because they cannot be accessed outside of the function, but they are more correctly thought of as shared private variables.

Now compare this to what happens if you call a Function more than once to produce multiple inner functions:

```
var myFunction = function () {
                var myVar = 1;
                return function (a) {
                        alert(myVar);
                        myVar++;
                };
        };
```

In this case myFunction returns a reference to a Function object that it creates. This is a more usual way for an inner function to persist after its outer function has finished running. The execution context of this function includes the variable myVar which the function displays and then increments.

What do you think you see if you try:

```
var myF1=myFunction();
var myF2=myFunction();
myF1();
myF1();
myF2();
myF2();
```

Notice that myF1 and myF2 are identical functions and they both increment myVar provided by the outer function – but is it the same myVar?

The answer is no.

You will see 1,2 followed by 1,2 rather than 1,2,3,4 because myF1 and myF2 each have their own copy of myVar. Each time myFunction is executed a new myVar is created along with a new execution context and hence a new closure. Once you realize that myVar is created anew each time myFunction is executed it becomes obvious that myF1 and myF2 cannot share the same variable.

An Example

Understanding the idea of a shared or non-shared execution context can help avoid errors such as:

```
var myFunction = function () {
                this.f = new Array(5);
                for (var i = 0; i < 5; i++) {
                  this.f[i] = function () {
                            alert(i);
                        };
            }
        };
```

The intention here is to create an array of five functions which when called displays the current value of i when the function was created.

Can you see what is wrong?

The execution context has the variable i in it, but it is shared between the five functions. When any of the functions are called it has the value 5 which is the last value it was assigned in myFunction. As a result if you try:

```
        myFunction();
        for (i = 0; i < 5; i++) {
            f[i]();
        }
```

You will see 5 displayed five times which is not what is required or perhaps expected.

There are various ways of making this work as required but in ES5 it is tricky. If you want to let each inner function capture the current value of i when the function is defined then you have little choice but to create a separate execution context for each of the inner functions.

The simplest way to do this is to introduce another function which creates the original inner functions:

```
var myFunction = function () {
                this.f = new Array(5);
                for (var i = 0; i < 5; i++) {
                  (function context() {
                      var j=i;
                      this.f[i] = function () {
                                  alert(j);
                      };
                  })();
                }
};
```

The overall plan of the code is much the same as before but now the function context constructs the inner functions. It declares a new variable j which is included in the execution context of the inner functions. Notice that the context function is executed immediately because of the final parentheses.

This means that the Function object corresponding to context is created and executed each time through the for loop. This creates a separate execution context for each of the inner functions each with their own version of variable j.

If this seems complicated – it is, and it is inefficient in that two Function objects are created each time through the loop.

ES2015 has a much easier solution – block scope.

Block Scope

JavaScript before ES2015 only supported function scope variables. That is, no matter where you declared a variable its scope was the entire Function it was declared in. Not only this but all variable declarations are hoisted to the top of the Function.

ES2015 introduces block scoped variables with the keywords let and const. The only difference between let and const is that, as its name suggests, a variable created using const cannot be reassigned.

A block is a compound statement enclosed by curly brackets and you can use let or const to declare variables that are in scope only within the block.

For example:

```
var myVar = 1;
alert(myVar);
{
    let myVar = 2;
    alert(myVar);
}
alert(myVar);
```

This displays 1 then 2 and then 1 again. Within the block myVar in the outer scope is no longer accessible as the block scope version of myVar is.

The same thing works with const but in this case you wouldn't be able to change the value of myVar once set.

Now we come to the question of hoisting.

Block scope variables are hoisted, but only to the start of their scope i.e. the block that contains them. They are also not initialized to undefined but left uninitialized. This might seem like a strange thing to do, but it is designed to block variables in the outer scope being accessible within the block before the block variable is declared.

For example:

```
var myVar = 1;
{
  alert(myVar);
  let myVar = 2;
  alert(myVar);
}
```

If it wasn't for the declaration of myVar within the block, the outer scoped myVar would be accessible within the block. You might think that the first alert would display the current value of the outer myVar but instead it generates a runtime error that tells you myVar isn't defined. This is because the declaration of let myVar is hoisted to the start of the block but the variable is left undefined until the code reaches the assignment.

Because of hoisting, block scope variables override outer scope variables of the same name throughout the block irrespective of where they are declared.

There is another very important difference between function and block scoped variables. You can declare a function scoped variable as often as you like and it has no effect:

```
var myVar=1;
var myVar=2;
```

is fine and equivalent to:

```
var myVar=1;
myVar=2;
```

However, you can only declare a block scope variable once:

```
{
  let myVar=1;
  let myVar=2;
}
```

generates a runtime error:

```
Identifier 'myVar' has already been declared
```

The same is true for const.

You might not be able to declare a block scoped variable twice, but you can declare one within a loop or in the head of a loop. In this case the declaration causes a new instance of the variable to be created. This means you can use a block scoped variable within a loop and use it to create a unique execution context each time.

For example we can write the example in the previous section much more simply using let:

```
var myFunction = function () {
                this.f = new Array(5);
                for (var i = 0; i < 5; i++) {
                  let j = i;
                  this.f[i] = function () {
                              alert(j);
                              };
                }
              };
```

This works and each function now gets its own instance of the variable j. You can also write the function as:

```
var myFunction = function () {
                this.f = new Array(5);
                for (let i = 0; i < 5; i++) {
                  this.f[i] = function () {
                              alert(i);
                              };
                }
              }
```

Again the execution context has a new instance of i each time through the loop. This also works with const. Notice that neither example works if you change let to var.

There are some other subtle behaviors caused by block scoping – for example block scoped top level variables are not global properties. It is also worth mentioning that function statements are also block scoped in ES2015 but hoisted in the usual way to the start of their scope.

Summary

- A Function object can be created by the evaluation of a function body. This is often described as nesting one function inside another, but it is important to realize that this nesting is really only about the way the contained function body can access variables in the containing function body.

- Like all JavaScript objects, a Function object exists until there are no references to it when it is automatically garbage collected.

- Variables declared within a function are local to that function and are created when the function is executed and destroyed when it ends. However, closures modify this behavior.

- All of the variables declared by any enclosing functions are in scope and can be accessed by an inner function body. This is called nested scope.

- All of the variables that are in scope when the Function object is created remain accessible whenever the function body is evaluated and this includes times when the relevant variables would have been destroyed by the normal rules. This is a closure.

- The idea of a closure is a natural consequence of using Function objects with differing lifetimes and nested scope.

- Each time a function is executed, an execution context is created and this is shared by all of the functions created by that function.

- The variables in the execution context all have their final value when accessed as part of a closure, but they can be changed. Hence they are privates shared variables.

- ES2015 introduces block scoped variables using let and const. These can be used to force a new execution context to be created.

Chapter 7

Parameters, Returns and Destructuring

In this short chapter we look at some of the more practical aspects of using Functions in JavaScript. There is nothing deep and philosophical about the ways that we can use JavaScript's functions, but it does give you some idea of how powerful the idea that "everything is an object" and weak typing are.

Object Parameters

Another big difference between JavaScript and most other languages is that parameters in functions and return values can be objects of any type – in fact it is easier to forget ideas of type and simply regard parameters as objects. This has the effect of also removing any ideas of function signature, i.e. the types of the parameters and hence of function overloading. If you are familiar with languages where both of these ideas are central to object-oriented programming, this will seem to be a big loss. However, what you have in return is the idea that a function can be written to deal with any objects that happen to be passed to it.

For example, in other languages you might well have to write a function to add two integers and another to add two floats. If you want a function that works with both integers and floats then you have to invent generics and deal all of the complications that this brings. In JavaScript you can simply write:

```
function add(a,b){
  return a+b;
}
```

and use the function to add two integers, or two decimal valued numbers, or even two strings, although in this case the result is concatenation rather than addition. What is more, you can pass any two objects to the add function without generating any compile time error.

For example:

```
alert(add({},{}));
```

There are no restrictions on what sort of object you can pass to a function as a parameter and no restriction on what the function can return.

This freedom can seem like an invitation to chaos but in there are many simplifications that also result. For example, there is no need to event the complex subject of generics because all JavaScript functions are generic.

The whole idea of typeless programming is taken up in later chapters, but this is where it first makes itself felt.

Arguments Object

The fact that parameters are objects is a powerful feature but, as mentioned in an earlier chapter, in fact the entire parameter list is an object.

Every function, apart from arrow functions, has a local arguments object which contains all of the parameter values passed to the function in something that looks like an Array. What is more, the function declaration does not determine what can be passed to the function at the point of use.

That is, function declarations do not need to specify any parameters at all and you can call any function with any list of arguments you care to use.

For example:

```
function sum(){
    var total=0;
    for(var i=0;i<arguments.length;i++){
        total+=arguments[i];
    }
    return total;
}
```

which will add any number of parameters you care to specify. Notice that the declaration does not specify anything at all about the parameters that the function expects.

You can call it using:

```
alert(sum(1,2,3,4));
```

or with any number of parameters of any type.

The arguments list is processed by the JavaScript engine to produce an object that is like an Array.

This is really all we need to write any function and indeed other languages struggle to provide this level of flexibility.

So why do we have a parameter list in function declarations?

The simple answer is to make JavaScript functions look more like functions in other languages and to make simple functions easier to write. Any parameter list that you specify in the declaration is used to deconstruct the arguments object into named local variables.

For example:

```
function sum(a,b,c){
}
```

unpacks the first three parameters you pass into a, b and c respectively. If you pass fewer than three then any parameters that do not have values are undefined. If you pass more than three then only the first three values are used in the local variables but of course all of the values are still available in the arguments object.

This unpacking or destructuring of the arguments object really is a good way to think about how parameters work in JavaScript. For example, there is a two way connection between the parameter variables and the arguments object. If you change the arguments object then the value in the variable changes and vice versa.

For example:

```
function myFunction(a){
    alert(a);
    arguments[0]=1;
    alert(a);
    a=2;
    alert(arguments[0]);
}
MyFunction(0);
```

displays 0, 1, 2 and changing arguments changes the associated parameters and vice versa.

Strict Mode

The association between arguments and parameters is broken in strict mode. Any changes to arguments do not change the parameters and vice versa.

Passing An Array To arguments – Spread

If parameters are passed to functions in the arguments array you might be wondering whether you can bypass the comma separated list of parameters and simply pass an Array that is used as arguments.

You can, but only if you call the array using either the apply method that every Function object has or you are prepared to use some new syntax introduced with ES2015.

First, to pass a parameter array in almost any version of JavaScript you can use apply:

```
function sum(a,b){return a+b;};
var args=[1,2];
sum.apply(null,args);
```

This passes the args array to the function as the arguments object which is then unpacked into the usual parameters.

Using the new ES2015 spread operator ... you can write the above as:

```
function sum(a,b){return a+b;};
var args=[1,2];
sum(...args);
```

The spread operator will unbundle any iterable object like an array and it works in function arguments, elements of array literals, and object expressions where key value pairs are needed.

Rest (ES2015)

You can find out how many parameters are specified in a function's declaration using the function's length property.

For example:

```
function sum(a,b,c){
}
```

```
sum.length
```

is 3.

This is the number of parameters specified in the declaration not the number of arguments in the use of the function.

Notice that using the function length and arguments length properties we can easily work out how many more or fewer arguments have been supplied.

For example:

```
function sum(a,b,c){
 var total=a+b+c;
    for(var i=sum.length;i<arguments.length;i++){
        total+=arguments[i];
    }
    return total;
}
```

This will add the first three arguments using the parameters a, b and c and if there are any more it adds them from the arguments object.

To make this sort of thing even easier ES2015 added the rest parameter. If the last parameter of a function is prefixed with ... then any additional arguments provided are stored in the final parameter as an Array.

So the previous function could be written:

```
function sum(a,b,c,...rest){
 var total=a+b+c;
    for(var i=0;i<rest.length;i++){
        total+=rest[i];
    }
    return total;
}
```

Notice that you don't have to call the final parameter rest, only the three dots matter. You don't need the rest feature but it is slightly easier.

Default Parameters (ES2015)

JavaScript is so flexible that often we allow optional parameters that are set to a default if the user doesn't make use of them. Obviously as JavaScript's parameters are positional, any optional parameters have to be last in the parameters list.

The traditional way of dealing with optional parameters is to test for undefined values. For example:

```
function add(a, b) {
    b = (typeof b !== 'undefined') ? b : 1;
    return a + b;
}
```

If you don't supply a value for b then it is set to 1.

ES2015 introduced default parameter values which work in much the same way. For example:

```
function add(a, b=1) {
    return a + b;
}
```

sets b to 1 if it isn't provided.

Notice that ES2015 default parameters are compiled to exactly the code given earlier. That is, if you pass in undefined then the default value will still be used but any other value including null etc, will not be replaced by the default. Also notice that the default value can be any valid expression including function calls, and this is evaluated each time the function is called. These default expression are evaluated in order of the parameters and earlier defaults can be used in later parameter defaults. For example:

```
function add(a=1,b=a+1){
```

b is set to a+1 if it isn't supplied.

Destructuring (ES2015)

Although destructuring is a general facility it has some particularly important uses in connection with functions and it can be seen as a generalization of the way the arguments object is unpacked or destructured into the parameter variables.

The basic idea of destructuring is that it will unpack the values in an array or the properties in an object into individual variables. The syntax is simply to assign to a structure of the same type but with variables rather than values. For example:

```
var a,b;
[a,b]=[1,2]
```

or

```
var [a,b]=[1,2];
```

assigns 1 to a and 2 to b. Notice that [1,2] is an array literal but the destructuring works with a general Array object.

Destructuring an object is very similar:

```
var {x:a,y:b}={x:1,y:2};
```

This assigns 1 to a and 2 to b. Notice that you have to use the property names to determine which property maps to which variable. For example:

```
var {y:a,x:b}={x:1,y:2};
```

assigns 2 to a and 1 to b.

As a shorthand you can destructure to variables with the same name as the properties. For example:

```
var {x,y}={x:1,y:2};
```

which is a short form of:

```
var {x:x,y:y}={x:1,y:2};
```

You should be able to see that Array destructuring is a lot like the way arguments are unpacked into the parameter variables and the similarity is more than skin deep.

For example, you don't have to unpack all of the elements of an Array, you can use the rest notation to set an Array to take any part of the source Array that isn't used and finally you can set default values.

For example:

```
var [a,b,c=3,...d]=[1,2];
```

assigns 1 to a, 2 to b, 3 to c and d is an Array of length 0 and:

```
var [a,b,c=3,...d]=[0,1,2,3,4,5];
```

assigns 0 to a, 1 to b, 2 to c and d is [3,4,5].. Notice that the default value is only used if the source element is undefined. Also keep in mind that default values can be arbitrary expressions that evaluate to objects.

Named Parameters

One of the things that JavaScript is sometime criticized for is its lack of named parameters. At first sight it only seems to support positional parameters, however, this isn't quite true.

As you can pass an object as a parameter you already have named parameters as properties of the object.

A common pattern is to use an options object. For example:

```
function myFunction(myOptions){
}
```

and the function is called using something like:

```
myFunction({myOption1:myvalue1,myOption2:myvalue2});
```

and so on, including all of the options you care to use. Within the function the options object is processed using tests to see if the allowed options have been set.

For example:

```
function myFunction(myOptions){
  myOptions = (typeof myOptions !== 'undefined') ? myOptions : {};
  var myOption1 = (typeof myOptions.myOption1 !== 'undefined') ?
                                     myOptions.myOptions1 : 1;
}
```

Notice that you do have to check that an options object was supplied at all as well as for each of the possible options.

The options object pattern provides named parameters and default values without any additions to ES5. Noticed also that each property can be an object in its own right so it is possible to create complex parameter systems.

With some help from ES2015 you can make named parameters even easier. The trick here is that if you write an object with just property names as a parameter then the argument assignment when the function is called is treated as a destructuring assignment.

For example:

```
function myFunction({myOption1=1,myOption2=2}){
}
```

looks like a set of default parameter values but it isn't, it is a destructuring assignment with default values. When you call the function using say:

```
myFunction({myOption1:3});
```

then when the parameter is assigned the argument you have effectively:

```
var {myOption1=1,myOption2=2}={myOption1:3};
```

and you can see that myOption1 gets assigned a value and myOption2 is assigned a default value.

Note that myOption1 and myOption2 are local variables within the function.

This form of named parameters with defaults fails if you don't pass an options object at all.

To avoid this problem all we need to do is use a default value for the parameter:

```
function myFunction({myOption1=1,myOption2=2}={}){
}
```

Now if you call myFunction using:

```
myFunction();
```

The parameter is set to {} as the default and the effective destructuring assignment is:

```
var {myOption1=1,myOption2=2}={};
```

which of course sets all of the myOption variables to their defaults.

Multiple Return Values

Some languages have the ability to return multiple values but JavaScript can only return a single value. However, as that value can be an object you can easily arrange to return multiple values without anything need being needed. For example:

```
function myFunction(){
  rest of function
 return {a:a,b:b};
}
```

Returns an object which contains the values stored in the variables a and b as properties called a and b.

In many case this is all that is needed and the calling program can simply work with the return object or unpack the values to variables as needed:

```
var obj=myFunction();
var a=obj.a;
var b=obj.b;
```

This works and it fairly easy but if you are prepared to use ES2015 then you can use destructuring again:

```
var {a,b}=myFunction();
```

This automatically unpacks the object into the variables a and b.

Destructuring used with the ability to return an object is equivalent to being able to return multiple values from a function.

Summary

- Function declarations do not specify the number or type of parameters a function expects. This makes all functions generic and function overloading is unnecessary.

- Any arguments that you specify when you call the function are packed into the arguments object which is an Array like object.

- You can work with the arguments object to access the parameter's value.

- If you want to pass an array of values to become the arguments object you can use the ES2015 spread operator ...

- You can set a final parameter to accept the part of the arguments object that wasn't unpacked using the rest operator ...

- If you do define parameters in the function declaration then the arguments object is destructured into them.

- You can use destructuring on other arrays and objects.

- ES2015 adds default values to parameters, which is exactly like the way you would have done it in ES5.

- You can use destructuring to add named parameters to JavaScript.

- Returning an object combined with destructuring is equivalent to being able to return multiple values from a function.

Chapter 8

How Functions Become Methods

So far we have looked at the role that the Function object plays in bringing executable code to JavaScript in general. Other languages have functions, methods or subroutines, but JavaScript has the Function object, which is a general object which has an additional default "code" property that can be evaluated using the evaluation or invocation operator ().

In this chapter, the aim is to show how Function objects are used as methods by other JavaScript objects. Central to this transformation is the `this` keyword.

What is a Method?

Before we look at how JavaScript deals with methods it is worth spending a few minutes looking at the general problem.

When we first started writing programs in higher-level languages, best practice was to write a function for whatever you needed to do.

For example, if you needed to sort an array, you would write a sort function which accepted a few parameters that determined the data and the operation:

```
sort(myArray,order);
```

Where myArray is the data that you want to sort and order is a parameter that sets the sort order to be used.

Later on we moved over to object-oriented programming where data and the functions that process the data are grouped together into entities called objects. In this case the functions like sort became methods of the data that they were to operate on.

So an Array object would have a sort method and you would write the sort operation as:

```
myArray.sort(order);
```

You can see that this is a small change from the use of myArray as a parameter to the sort function to myArray as an object and sort method. You could say that the whole of the shift from functions to object-oriented programming is all about the shift of a parameter from inside the function to outside.

111

Looking a little deeper the simplification that this shift brings about is well worth it.

The sort function can now use the data in myArray more or less by default and this makes it possible to create an isolation from the rest of the program. It also brings about a complete change in the way that we think about functions.

For example, you could say that myArray "knows how" to sort itself. Another object myList, say, may also "know how" to sort itself using its own sort function which isn't the same as the Array sort function.

This means that each data structure can have its own sort function and we can avoid having to have an arraySort function and a listSort function and so on.

This is a limited form of polymorphism and it is one of the huge advantages of object-oriented programming. Yet it is strange that even the most enthusiastic object-oriented programmers don't think that there is any problem in having overloaded functions to deal with different data types which is a problem much better solved by polymorphism. It is much better to have the data determine which function to use rather than the signature of a detached function.

Now let's look at the different ways that objects and functions work together in JavaScript.

Objects With Function Properties

As we discovered in Chapter 2, an object is a set of properties with object values. As a function is nothing more than a Function object, there is no reason why a function cannot be a property of another object.

For example:

```
var myObject={myFunction: function(){alert("My Function");}};
```

creates a new object with a single property myFunction which is a Function object with code body:

```
alert("My Function");
```

The only problem with defining Function properties is how to format them on the page to make the code clear.

Most use something like:

```
var myObject={
    myFunction: function(){
                alert("My Function");
                }
};
```

To execute the code body of the Function property you simply need a reference to the Function object and the property i.e.:

```
myObject.myFunction
```

and the evocation operator () which gives:

```
myObject.myFunction();
```

And it is always worth remembering the difference between the two.

If there were parameters they would be included in the usual way between the parentheses.

You can also write:

```
myObject["myFunction"];
```

as the reference to the Function object and:

```
myObject["myFunction"]();
```

as the evaluation of the function body. In this form it looks a lot less like a traditional function call but there is nothing new here either.

Why would you use an object with Function properties?

Namespaces

An object is a good way to gather together functions that do the same sort of job.

For example, the built-in Math object provides a place to group mathematical functions like sin, cos and so on. To use such a function you have to write something like:

```
var ans=Math.sin(0.5);
```

In this case it might seem inconvenient to have to write the full "dotted" reference to the Function object, but in general it is useful to be able to separate the name applied to this function and any other function which might happen to have the same name.

In other words, using Functions within objects is a way of avoiding name collisions.

Whenever you are working on a large program trying to find unique names for things becomes increasingly difficult as the program gets bigger. You generally end up applying a good name to the first function or variable of a particular type such as totalHours, only later to have to use something less meaningful such as tHours to avoid the name collision with the first function or variable.

In other languages name collisions are made less of a problem by the use of "namespaces" which assign multi-part names for things without having to get involved in creating objects necessarily. Usually the first part of the name is derived by the IDE or the language conventions unless there is a name collision when you have to provide a fully qualified name.

Objects are often used in JavaScript as namespaces just like the Math object. If you want to create an alternative function called sin then you can because the built-in sin's full name is Math.sin.

Of course to avoid a name collision with someone else's sin function you would be well advised to put your new function within a suitable object - e.g. myMathFunctions. Of course the trick here is finding a name for your "namespace" object that is going to be unique and so avoid an initial name collision. This is the reason why some programs make use of a domain name for the object e.g. iprogrammerinfo but this is usually unnecessary and makes things look complicated.

You can also make use of multiple nested objects to create a nested namespace. So you could have:

```
myMath.trig.sin
```

or:

```
myMath.optimize.linear
```

and so on.

JavaScript doesn't have explicit support for namespaces and so using objects as namespaces makes good sense.

You can even simplify naming where required by assigning the fully qualified name to something shorter. For example:

```
var sin=Math.sin;
```

and following this statement you can just write:

```
var result=sin(0.5);
```

To labor the point for one final time, notice that Math.sin isn't a function, it is a reference to a Function object that is one of the properties of the Math object.

Functions Become Methods

You might at this point be thinking that we have just looked at how an object can have methods – this isn't so.

An object can have Functions as properties, and this is useful, but a simple Function object even when assigned as a property isn't a method.

Why not?

The reason is that a method is something that an object does to itself.

That is, the code of a method doesn't just do something external like compute a sin or a square root. A method is something that you ask an object to do like print itself, or use its data properties to make a connection to a secure server, or copy itself.

A method is an action that an object performs which involves other parts of the object.

Yes, the definition is vague and you could argue that a collection of math functions were methods but the best test of whether a function is a method is to ask if it would work in the same way if you removed it from its object. That is Math.sin(0.5) can be considered to work in the same way and do the same job as sin(0.5).

Now consider a something like:

```
myObject.size();
```

which returns the size of the object computed in some way appropriate to the object. Ask yourself what does:

```
size();
```

mean when it is removed from the object? Clearly by our definition size() is a method as it needs to know the object it is a property of to do its job.

At this point you may object slightly and point out that you can convert size the method into size the function by providing it with a parameter. That is:

```
myObject.size();
```

is the same as:

```
size(myObject);
```

both of which return the size of the object in some appropriate way.

Yes absolutely right and it's not really an objection.

As described earlier this swapping of object property to parameter is the key to the difference between a method and a pure function.

For a function to be a method it has to accept the object it belongs to as some sort of default parameter – and this is where "this" comes in.

In JavaScript this is a variable that is provided to every Function object that references the object involved in calling the function.

The Problem

Consider for a moment a simple example of a function as an object property:

```
var myObject = { mySize: 99,
                 getSize: function() {
                      return mySize;
                 }
              };
```

You can see what it is trying to do.

The getSize function is to return the size of the object as given by the object's mySize property.

If you try this out using say:

```
alert(myObject.getSize());
```

you will discover that you get an error message telling you that mySize is not defined. This is perfectly reasonable as mySize in the function's body either is a reference to a local or a global variable and clearly neither exist.

To make the function into a proper working method we have to make mySize reference the property of the object called mySize.

We can do this very easily and in the obvious, in fact far too obvious way using:

```
return myObject.mySize;
```

This works but it isn't a good way of achieving the result we are looking for. Using the name of the object in a method isn't a good idea at all.

The reason is that myObject isn't the name of the object in question. It just happens to be a variable that references the object at the moment.

Consider:

```
var myObject = { mySize: 99,
                 getSize: function() {
                    return myObject.mySize;
                 }
              };
var myOtherObject=myObject;
var myObject={};
alert(myOtherObject.getSize());
```

All that happens here is that we set another variable to reference the object and use the original variable for something else i.e. to store an empty object.

Now the program still runs but the size is returned as undefined.

This is the problem that we encountered in Chapter 5 – objects are anonymous.

You can't make use of the object's name in a method because the object doesn't have a name only variables that reference it, and these can change at any time.

When we looked at this problem in connection with Function objects the solution was to use callee or construct a self variable. When it comes to methods JavaScript provides a solution in the form of this.

The Solution – this

The solution to the problem of how to reference the object that the method is a property of is a very simple one – the call context.

When you evaluate a Function object that is a property of an object, the built-in variable "this" is set to reference the same object.

That is, when you write:

```
myObject.getSize();
```

this is set to reference the same object as myObject by the system. If you write:

```
myOtherObject.getSize();
```

"this" is set to reference the same object as myOtherObject no matter what that object might be.

So what this means is you can now write the getSize method as:

```
function(){
  return this.mySize;
}
```

Now when you write:

```
myObject.getSize();
```

this is set to the same object as myObject and the method is equivalent to:

```
function() {
  return myObject.mySize;
}
```

and all without actually using the myObject variable in the code.

If you use this in the method's code then it clearly doesn't matter what variable you use to reference the object as this will reference the same object.

Simple, elegant and it works – as long as you understand it and use it properly.

In Chapter 2 is was stated that outside of a function `this` references the Global object and now you can see that this is logical. Outside of a function the Global object is the object that can be considered to call all the other functions.

When a Function object is called as the property of another object then `this` **is set to reference that object.**

When a Function object is called not as a property of another object then `this` **is set to the global object.**

There is an important subtlety here.

Function Objects Are Late Bound

A Function object exists in its own right and not as part of some other object.

When you create a Function object as a property of another object the Function object exists as an independent entity and how it is evaluated depends on how it is used. A Function object can have many references to it and some of these might be as properties of another object and some might be global.

Whether a Function object is treated as a function or a method depends on how you reference it.

For example:

```
var myObject = { mySize: 99,
                getSize: function() {
                        return this.mySize;
                    }
            };

var myFunction=myObject.getSize;
```

The Function object the getSize property references is created when the object that myObject references is created – but it is just a normal object that happens to be a Function object. The second statement of the program sets myFunction to reference that same Function object.

Now if you call the function using:

```
myObject.getSize();
```

`this` references the same object that myObject references and so the function works correctly as a method bound to myObject.

If you call the function using:

```
myFunction();
```

`this` will be set to reference the Global object and in this case the function will be evaluated as if all its variables were global. In this case, of course, the function will not work because there is no global variable called mySize.

The point is that Function objects exist independently of other objects and as a result a given Function object can be a method bound to an object when called in one way and not a bound method when called in another.

Yet another way of putting this is that Function objects are late bound to any objects that might use them as methods i.e. what this references is only determined when the function is evaluated and it can change dynamically.

This is often quoted as a defect of JavaScript because in other languages functions are always methods that are bound to instances of classes. They always belong to a particular object and this always, well nearly always, means the same object for all time.

Now consider the situation with JavaScript.

A Function object always has an independent existence from any other object. It can therefore be evaluated in its own right and this will be set to the global object in our example. In this case this is usually a problem!

It can also be evaluated as a property of any other object and this will then be set to reference that object.

A Function object can also be a method for lots of different objects at the same time. Of course all of those objects have to have at least the properties that the function makes use of or the function has to test for the existence of those properties before it makes use of them.

Shared Instance Methods

The fact that any Function object can be a method makes it possible to share methods between objects. In JavaScript, unlike most class-based languages, methods are not shared by default between objects no matter how similar they are. That is, if myObject1 has a getSize method and myObject2 has a getSize method defined in the usual way then each has its own Function object:

```
var myObject1={
            sizeInBytes:1,
            size:function(){
                return this.sizeInBytes;
                }
            };
var myObject2={
            sizeInBytes:1,
            size:function(){
                return this.sizeInBytes;
                }
            };
```

Each Function object has its own code, properties, own execution context and so on.

If you have only one or two objects using getSize this is a small overhead to pay for the simplicity. Sometimes, however, it would be better to create a single Function object and reuse it. In this case the Function object has to be created as if it was a method i.e. it has to use this and it is also a good idea to add checks that the properties it makes use of actually exist.

For example consider the following function object:

```
function getSize(){
   return this.sizeInBytes;
}
```

If you just call this function then it will return the global variable sizeInBytes assuming there is one, or you will see a runtime error.

You can easily protect the function from runtime errors of this sort by testing for a valid this and a valid property:

```
function getSize(){
    if (typeof this === 'undefined') return 0;
    if (typeof this.sizeInBytes === 'undefined') return 0;
    return this.sizeInBytes;
}
```

You can now use this as a method in any object that needs it, i.e. that has a sizeInBytes property:

```
var myObject1={
    sizeInBytes:1,
    size:getSize
};
var myObject2={
    sizeInBytes:2,
    size:getSize
};
```

and you can use it in the usual way:

```
alert(myObject1.size());
alert(myObject2.size());
```

Notice that you can add this function to any object that needs the method, resulting in those objects sharing the same Function object. The method gets a new value of this and all its local variables are recreated each time it is used so it behaves like an instance method. However, if you define properties on the Function object which the code makes use of, then the properties are shared between all of the object instances that make use of the Function object, and hence behave more like static or class properties.

The usual way of sharing a Function object between instances is to use the prototype mechanism which is discussed in detail in Chapter 10. However, this is a perfectly good way to achieve the same result and sometimes it has the advantage of not being involved in the prototype chain.

Call and Apply

As discussed a method is a function that is supplied with a default parameter – the object that it is bound to – in `this`. Usually you can let the JavaScript engine automatically supply the value of `this` but occasionally it doesn't work as you might expect. If you want to call a method with a fixed value of `this` – i.e. as a function rather than a method, then you can use the `call` and `apply` methods of the Function object.

If you use:

```
function.call(thisarg,args)
```

then the function will be evaluated with `this` set to thisarg and the parameters set to the values specified as the comma separated list args. As we are currently interested in the distinction between methods and functions we can ignore the args for the moment as they are optional.

For example, if you define the Function object we used in the previous section as a method:

```
var getSize= function() {
            return this.mySize;
        }
```

you can use it as an ad-hoc method for any object using `call`. For example:

```
getSize.call(myObject);
```

evaluates getSize with `this` set to myObject. In other words, you get the same result as if getSize was a method of myObject i.e. it will try to access myObject.mySize.

If you think back to the introduction to this chapter and the explanation of the basic principle of object-oriented programming you can see that call is the link between the two ways to call a function – as a function which operates on some data:

```
sort.call(myArray,order);
```

and calling it as a method:

```
myArray.sort(order);
```

You can also use apply in the same way; the only difference is that after the thisarg you can supply an array of values to be used as arguments for the function's parameters.

The two methods call and apply allow you to borrow methods from other objects by calling them with set values for this.

Early and Late Binding – the Bind Method

It should be clear from the description of how the `this` mechanism works that JavaScript implements a late binding of methods to objects. That is, the object that `this` references is only determined when the function is actually called. Other languages implement an early binding mechanism where the object reference is determined at compile time.

JavaScript's late binding of Function objects isn't usually a problem – except when it is.

The fact that Functions are objects means that you can pass a function as a parameter, assign it as a property and so on. However, all of these actions result in you passing or assigning a function object, not a method, and sometimes we want to manipulate a method.

For example, earlier we created a method:

```
var myObject = { mySize: 99,
            getSize: function() {
                  return this.mySize;
            }
      };
```

but when the method is assigned to another variable:

```
var myFunction=myObject.getSize;
```

it reverts to being just a Function object when called as:

```
myFunction();
```

Can we do this in a way that makes myFunction a method bound to myObject?

In other words can we arrange to early bind the Function object to myObject, and the answer is yes.

If you are using ES5 and an up-to-date browser then the simplest way is to use the `bind` method of the Function object:

```
function.bind(object)
```

This creates a copy of the Function object with `this` permanently set to the object you specify.

If you are not using ES5 there are various well known "polyfills" that do the same job using the apply method.

Using bind is very simple. For example:

```
var myFunction=myObject.getSize.bind(myObject);
```

creates a copy of getSize with this set to myObject for all time. That is, this is bound to myObject well before the function is evaluated i.e. this is early binding. Now if you evaluate myFunction:

```
myFunction();
```

you will get the result 99 as determined by the state of myObject. That is, myFunction is actually a reference to a method of myObject.

One subtlety to be aware of, although it rarely causes any problems, is that the myFunction references a new Function object, which evaluates the original unbound function using apply. The object it is bound to, i.e. the new Function object referenced by myFunction, is something like:

```
var myFunction=function(){
                return myObject.getSize.apply(myObject);
            }
```

This means that the new Function object doesn't have any of the properties of the original Function object, but this usually doesn't matter as most Function objects don't have any additional custom properties.

In most of the examples you will come across, bind is used in an ad-hoc manner, to convert a function into a method, as in the example above.

You can also use the bind method to create early bound methods as properties of objects.

That is, objects can have late and early bound methods.

For example:

```
var myObject = {mySize: 99};
myObject.getSize=function() {
                    return this.mySize;
                }.bind(myObject);
```

This creates a method early bound to myObject right from its definition. Notice that you can't define the function in the object literal as previously done because myObject, which you need to specify in the bind, isn't defined until the literal is fully defined. That is, you can't use myObject within the definition of myObject.

With this slight change you can now do things like:

```
var myMethod=myObject.getSize;
```

and when you evaluate myMethod() it will return the value in myObject.

This idiom of creating early bound methods as object properties is preferable to converting a late bound method into an early bound reference, because there is only one Function object involved, complete with any properties you create.

The Onclick Example

The best known example, or is it complaint, about JavaScript's late binding is the mistake many beginners make when assigning an event handler that is also a method.

For example:

```
var myObject = {mySize: 99};
myObject.getSize=function() {
                alert(this.mySize);
             };
Button1.onclick=myObject.getSize;
```

Notice that assigning the Function object to a property of Button1 makes it a method of Button1 as well as of myObject – this is an example of one Function object serving two masters in that it is a method of myObject and Button1.

When you click the Button the Function is evaluated with this referencing the HTMLElement that is the Button. That is, in this case the Function object is bound to the Button object.

The result is that the getSize function doesn't work and the beginner wastes a lot of time trying to debug the code. This is also how JavaScript gets a bad name.

Of course the correct way to do the job is to early bind the method:

```
myObject.getSize=function() {
                alert(this.mySize);
             }.bind(myObject);
```

With the addition of just bind(myObject) the event handler now works as the novice expects and displays the value of myObject.mySize.

A better way is to early bind the method when assigning it as the event handler:

```
Button1.onclick=myObject.getSize.bind(myObject);
```

It sometimes matters if methods are late or early bound – it all depends how you plan to use them. When you create a method, early bind it to the object if you know that it will never be used with any other object, including instances created by a constructor. If this isn't the case then early bind the method if you allow another object to make use of it as in the case of the Button and the event handler method.

Overriding Object Methods

Another important use of the bind method is that it can be used to override methods in object instances. If an object already has a method called myMethod then simply redefining it overrides it.

That is:

```
myObject.myMethod=function(){....};
```

overrides the existing myMethod and substitutes the new function.

This works but often you want to make use of the old definition of myMethod to implement the new version.

How can you do this?

A simple minded approach would try to use something like:

```
var oldMyMethod=myObject.myMethod;
```

However, this doesn't work because when you try to call the old method this is set incorrectly. That is:

```
oldMyMethod();
```

calls the old version of MyMethod with this set to the global scope, usually window.

The trick is to use bind to retain the correct call context:

```
oldMyMethod=myObject.myMethod.bind(myObject);
```

Now a call to oldMyMethod() really does call the method with this set to myObject.

You can use this technique to override methods with code that calls the old method to get the job done.

Arrow Functions and this ES2015

Although arrow functions create Function objects in the usual way they don't follow the same behavior with regard to this. An arrow function uses the value of this that is current in its context when it is declared and the Function object is created.

You can say that arrow functions don't have a this but it is better to say that they don't have a this of their own.

Notice that this is subtle because as an arrow function doesn't have a this of its own, the this that is current when it is declared is part of its execution context and included in its closure.

For example, if we define myObject as:

```
var myObject = {mySize: 99,
                getSize:  ()=>{return this.mySize}
               };
```

Notice that the arrow function creates a Function object when myObject is created and at that point this is set to the global object. The this value is included in the closure and when you call the method this will still be the global object.

For example:

```
alert(myObject.getSize());
```

displays undefined unless there is a global variable called mySize.

If you declare an arrow function within a method defined in the usual way then the arrow function will have the same this as the method. If you think of arrow functions as lightweight utilities then this achieves exactly what you want.

For example:

```
var myObject = {mySize:99,
                getSize:function () {
                        var myArrow = () => {return this.mySize;};
                        return myArrow();
                    }
               };
```

In this case myArrow is declared within the method so the value of this will be whatever it is in the method call and:

```
alert(myObject.getSize());
```

now works because this is set to myObject when the arrow function creates its Function object. When myArrow is executed this is still set to myObject.

As the this is included in the closure it doesn't matter when myArrow is executed and it could be long after the method has finished executing. For example:

```
var myObject = {mySize: 99,
                getSize: function () {
                        var myArrow = () => {return this.mySize;};
                        setTimeout(function(){alert(myArrow());}
                                                      ,1000);

                    }
               };
```

99 will still be displayed even though myArrow isn't called until one second after the setTimeout is executed and the getSize method has finished executing.

Is the JavaScript Way Better?

JavaScript is certainly different and trying to make it look like the way other languages do the job is a big part of its problem.

The need to use a call context, i.e. `this`, is a consequence of treating functions as first class objects, which is very worthwhile. Function objects live longer than the period in which their code is being executed. As a result, converting them to methods with a default object reference is slightly more difficult. Sometimes you want the method to be always bound to the same object, in which case you need to manually apply early binding. If you want the method to work with a range of objects specified at call time then you need late binding which is the default if you use the call context `this`. You have great flexibility in how Function objects become methods.

JavaScript takes an approach that has a synergy in that all of the parts fit together and, yes, gives you more than the sum of the parts.

As long as you understand all of the parts.

Summary

- Functions are just objects and can be properties of other objects.

- A method is a function property that makes use of the object it is a property of in its code.

- To allow a method to reference the object it is a property of, it is passed an execution context in `this` – which is a reference to the object involved in the function call.

- Functions that are methods use `this.myProperty` to reference properties of the object they are bound to.

- A Function object exists independently of any object that it is a property or method of. This means it can be referenced by other variables and the object it is bound to depends on how the function is called. A single Function object can be a method for many different objects and it can be just a Function object.

- You can use `apply` and `call` to explicitly set the value of `this` and so borrow methods from other objects and create ad-hoc methods that aren't properties of the object that they work with.

- By default JavaScript methods are late bound to their objects.

- The `bind` method can be used to create a Function object bound to any specified object.

- You can early bind a method to an object using `bind`

- In general you should use the default late bound method unless you need to assign or pass a method rather than a function when you should early bind.

Chapter 9

Object Creation

Object creation is fundamental to all object-oriented languages, but in JavaScript it is left to the programmer to work out how best to do it, and often the practice that you encounter isn't the best because it's borrowed from other languages.

One of the most misunderstood parts of JavaScript is the way that objects are created. The reason is that JavaScript doesn't make use of the idea of class, and programmers coming from other languages try to re-implement it. In a language that uses only object instances, reinventing class is a bit of a waste of time.

A class facility was introduced in ES2015, but this is only a very light wrapper for one of the ways of creating new instances with a form of inheritance. You can do exactly the same thing in ES5 without using the new facilities. The ES2015 approach is described in detail in Chapter 10.

Also the idea that JavaScript is a "prototype-based" language is also misleading. The prototype is often introduced as a way of creating object hierarchies as in a class-based language, but it has a much simpler purpose.

So how do we create objects in JavaScript?

If you already know about JavaScript constructors read on, because how they are arrived at is an important story.

The Classical Constructor

It might help to look first at how class-based languages deal with the problem of creating instances. If you don't know about how class-based languages work, just skip to the next section.

In class-based languages, instances of a class are generally created using the constructor, which implicitly uses the class definition to manufacture an instance of the class.

For example, in language like Java, C++ or C# you would write:

```
MyClass myObject = new myClass();
```

where myClass() is the constructor.

The constructor is a function that returns an instance of the class.

This is a fact that is often overlooked by programmers in class-based languages because they don't actually have to write anything in the constructor for it to do its job. That is, an empty or default constructor will automatically do the job of creating an instance. This results in programmers thinking that constructors are really only needed when something has to be initialized or set up in some way.

The idea of a constructor can be extended to the idea of an object factory. An object factory is an object that will create another object – perhaps another instance of its own type or another completely different type.

The idea of a function which creates objects is core to class-based languages and, in fact, to all object-oriented languages.

The JavaScript Object Factory

If you just want a single object then you could simply make use of an object literal and define your object.

For example:

```
var myObject={prop1:object1,prop2:object2... }
```

This works perfectly well and it is a good way to make a singleton object, i.e. an object that there should only be one instance of, in any given program. Surprisingly, singletons are the most common case of objects in most programs.

For example, if you want to store the position of a single 2D point you might define:

```
var myPoint={x:0,y:0};
```

However, if you want more than one copy of an object you need to automate the creation or implement a method of cloning an existing object. Although cloning is a perfectly proper way to create new instances of objects, it isn't the most usual way of going about the task. In JavaScript the standard practice is to use an object factory, and to be more precise a constructor. Let's take a look at the object factory approach first and then see how it specializes into a constructor.

An object factory is any function that returns a single object as its result. As a function in JavaScript is just an executable object, it sometimes helps to think of an object factory as an object that creates an instance of another object.

How do object factories work?

At their very simplest an object factory creates an object literal and returns it as its result.

For example an object factory for the point object is:

```
var Point=function(){
        return {x:0,y:0};
    };
```

and to use it to create an instance of the Point object you would use:

```
var myPoint=Point();
```

It seems trivial yet in no time at all it can become complicated and subtle.

Notice that we already have recreated one of the minor problems of a class-based language - finding a name for the class and for an instance. In this case the naming problem is finding something to call the object factory and then names for the instances - i.e. Point and myPoint. Perhaps it would be better to call the factory PointMaker or something to indicate that it wasn't actually an instance of a Point object.

As the object being created gets bigger and more complicated, building it in smaller steps becomes a better method. Starting from an empty object you can add properties one by one.

For example:

```
var Point=function(){
        var obj={};
        obj.x=0;
        obj.y=0;
        return obj;
    };
```

One of the big advantages of using an object factory is that you can use parameters to customize the object produced.

For example:

```
var Point=function(x,y){
        var obj={};
        obj.x=x;
        obj.y=y;
        return obj;
};
```

and you create the object using:

```
var myPoint=Point(1,2);
```

The ability to customize object instances is one of the big plus points of using an object factory. It is so useful that an object factory is often used to create a singleton – even though the factory will only ever create a single object.

Constructing Methods

Of course the object that the factory produces can have any type of object as its properties including Function objects.

As already explained in Chapter 8 function properties aren't really the same thing as methods.

To make a Function property act like a method you have to make use of the this call context, i.e. this, to specify the instance that is being referenced.

If you are creating an object as an object literal there is no other choice but to use this to create a late bound method for an object.

However, if you are using a factory function there is an alternative and it is arguably better as it creates an early bound method.

For example, suppose we want to write a method that adds x and y together:

```
var Point=function(x,y){
          var obj={};
          obj.x=x;
          obj.y=y;
          obj.add=function(){
                   return obj.x+obj.y;
               };
          return obj;
        };
```

Notice that the function uses obj.x and obj.y not just x and y.

If you try out:

```
var myPoint=Point(1,2);
myPoint.x=4;
alert(myPoint.add());
```

you will find it works and displays 6 – but how can it?

Private Variables

When myPoint.add is called, the variable obj has long gone as the factory object's code has terminated and all its variables have been destroyed. How can a Function object make use of the factory's obj variable long after it has been destroyed?

The answer, of course, is closure.

If you recall, closure in JavaScript is necessary to resolve the problem of having Function objects which live for longer than their code. When you define the add Function object it captures the variables that are in scope at the time of its creation, i.e. obj. Thus the add function has access to obj even though, without closure, it should have been destroyed.

Also notice that code in other Function objects can't access the obj variable because it no longer exists and it is local to the factory function. That is, obj is a private variable for the instance of the point object we have created.

The general rule is that any local variables declared within the object factory are turned into private variables for the object created by closure.

More exactly all of the methods created are assigned the same execution context as a closure. This means that all of the methods share the same private variables which is usually what you would expect and require.

This is another advantage of using an object factory even for a singleton. Object literals don't have private variables unless they are created within a function.

Private Properties

It should be obvious now that closure can be used to create private properties for objects, but it is worth exploring a little more.

For example, you can create a private property for the point object using something like:

```
var Point=function(x,y){
        var obj={};
        var myPrivateData=10;
        obj.getPriv= function(){
                return myPrivateData;
            };
        return obj;
    };
var myPoint= Point(1,2);
alert(myPoint.getPriv());
```

Where the code has been stripped down to just what is needed to demo a private variable. In this case the getPriv function can access myPrivateData because of closure and so everything works. However, any attempt to directly access the variable fails because there is no closure in operation and it is not a property of the constructed object.

That is both:

```
alert(myPoint.myPrivateData);
```

and:

```
alert(myPrivateData);
```

fail.

You can of course use a getter and setter with a private variable but it is slightly more complicated to add them using an object factory.

For example:

```
var Point=function(x,y){
          var obj={
                    get Priv(){return myPrivateData;}
               };
          var myPrivateData=10;
          return obj;
     };
```

Now you can use Priv as if it was a variable but there is no access to myPrivate data except through get or set:

```
var myPoint= Point(1,2);
alert(myPoint.Priv);
```

The private variable pattern is well known, but it works for methods as well although not as commonly.

For example, if you want to create a private function that only the object can use, all you have to do is declare it as a local variable within the object factory:

```
Point=function(x,y){
     var myPrivateData=10;
     var obj={};
     var myPrivateAdd=function(a,b){
                         return a+b;
                    };
     obj.add=function(){
             return myPrivateAdd(1,2);
          };
   };
```

In this case myPrivateAdd is accessible from the object constructed because of closure, which means it can be called from within any method of the object. Again the myPrivateAdd function cannot be called outside the object because it is not a property and is only available as a closure inside the object.

Notice that a private function can make use of private variables as these are made available to it by closures within the object itself.

The private variables and functions are instance entities in the sense that each object that the factory function produces has its own copy of all of the private entities because, as already explained, the execution context is created each time the factory function is used.

That is, all of the private variables are not shared.

If you want to make a private method, then you can use the obj variable within the private function to access properties of the object.

For example:

```
var Point = function (x, y) {
            var obj = {};
            obj.x = x;
            obj.y = y;
            var myPrivateAdd = function () {
                        return obj.x + obj.y;
            };
            obj.add = function () {
                   return myPrivateAdd();
                  };
            return obj;
      };
```

You can see that myPrivateAdd is private and can be used by the add method to add two properties of the Point object. This is a private method.

Using this

In the previous example we made use of a private variable to store a reference to the object being created. This allowed the methods of the object to refer to its properties.

You could have achieved more-or-less the same result using this as when you create an object literal.

For example:

```
var Point=function(x,y){
          var obj={};
          obj.x=x;
          obj.y=y;
          obj.add=function(){
                    return this.x+this.y;
                 };
          return obj;
        };
```

If you try this out you will find that it give the same result as using the private variable obj. That is:

```
var myPoint=Point(1,2);
myPoint.x=4;
alert(myPoint.add());
```

works and displays the answer 6 as before.

However, this works in a very different way from the private variable obj.

When you call the method:

```
myPoint.add();
```

the system sets this to reference the same object as myPoint and hence when the code is obeyed an expression like this.x is the same thing as myPoint.x which is what you want.

You can see that the private variable obj is an alternative to using this and perhaps obj isn't a good name to use for it. However, it has emphasized the fact that it isn't anything special and just a reference to the object instance that the factory object is creating.

To make the similarity between obj and this clearer you could use the name self, which is commonly used to make a self reference in other languages.

```
var Point=function(x,y){
          var self={};
          self.x=x;
          self.y=y;
          self.add=function(){
                   return self.x+self.y;
                };
          return self;
       };
```

Keep in mind that self isn't a keyword like this, it is just another variable. It is also important to note that this doesn't work in private methods. For example:

```
var Point = function (x, y) {
          var obj = {};
          obj.x = x;
          obj.y = y;
          var myPrivateAdd = function () {
                         return this.x + this.y;
                };
          obj.add = function () {
                   return myPrivateAdd();
                };
          return obj;
       };
```

Now if you make use of add you will see an undefined variable message:

```
alert(myPoint.add());
```

The reason is, of course that while this is set to myPoint in the call to add it isn't in the call to myPrivateAdd. This is another example of late binding causing problems. The solution is to either early bind the function, see the next section, or to use the call method:

```
obj.add = function () {
          return myPrivateAdd.call(this);
       };
```

Late and Early Binding

As with objects created as object literals, using `this` to convert a Function property into a method produces a late bound method.

That is, the association between the Function object and the object it is a property of is only established at runtime.

You can see that this is true if you create another reference to the Function object:

```
Point=function(x,y){
        var self={};
        self.x=x;
        self.y=y;
        self.add=function(){
                    return this.x+this.y;
                };
        return self;
        };
```

In the case:

```
var myPoint=Point(1,2);
myPoint.x=4;
var myFunc=myPoint.add;
alert(myFunc());
```

the new variable myFunc references the same function object as myPoint's add property. However, when called as myFunc this is set to the calling context which in this case is the global object. Now when the function tries to evaluate this.x or this.y it looks for global variables of the same name and there aren't any. This is why the result is NaN (Not a Number).

Now consider using a local private variable created by closure in place of `this`:

```
Point=function(x,y){
        var self={};
        self.x=x;
        self.y=y;
        self.add=function(){
                    return self.x+obj.y;
                };
        return self;
        };
```

Now when you try the same thing:

```
var myPoint=Point(1,2);
myPoint.x=4;
var myFunc=myPoint.add;
alert(myFunc());
```

the value of the local call context doesn't come into it. Now all that matters is what the obj variable references and this is always the object created by the object factory – hence the result is 6.

If you use a local variable in place of `this` in creating methods within an object factory the result is early bound methods.

If you use **`this`** the result is late bound methods.

Constructors

Object factories are a completely general idea.

You write a function that returns an object. JavaScript has some features which are specifically defined to make object factories more useful and perhaps easier to use.

A constructor is an object factory that you use in conjunction with the operator **new**.

For example:

```
var myPoint=new Point(1,2);
```

Using a constructor makes JavaScript look much more like other object-oriented languages which tend to use new and a class-based constructor.

What difference does the use of **new** in front of an object factory make?

There are quite a few differences. The first and most important is that when the object factory is called **`this`** isn't set to the call context but to a newly created empty object.

You can think of **new** as adding:

```
this={};
```

to the start of the object factory.

What this means is that instead of having to write:

```
var obj={};
```

or:

```
var self={}
```

you can just use **`this`** as a reference to the newly created empty object.

Another important change is that a constructor automatically returns **this** as a reference to the object that has been created.

For example, if we use a constructor to create a point object then the code would be:

```
Point=function(x,y){
        this.x=x;
        this.y=y;
        this.add=function(){
                    return this.x+this.y;
                };
        };
```

This works in the same way as our plane object factory version except for the fact that you have to put new in front when you use it. For example:

```
var myPoint=new Point(1,2);
```

Notice that in the constructor this has two distinct meanings.

The first is when it is used to refer to the object being constructed, for example:

```
this.x=x;
```

The second is when it appears within a method definition, for example:

```
return this.x+this.y;
```

As the code within a method definition isn't being executed, the current value of this has no effect. When the code is executed, this in the method is set to the call context and everything works.

Constructor Pitfalls

This double use of this in a constructor is often confusing to beginners. It also has the potential to cause some errors.

For example, if you use a constructor without new, then this is set to the current call context and not to a new empty object. The result is that the properties and methods that should have been added to the new object are added to the current call context. In most cases the call context is the global object, so all of the properties and methods are added to the global object.

For example:

```
var myPoint=Point(1,2);
x=4;
alert(add());
```

works because the constructor called without new adds x, y and add to the global object.

The hijacking of the `this` call context in the constructor also causes problems when `new` is used and for some reason the constructor wants to use the call context. This very rarely happens because constructors are not usually methods of other objects, however, they can be.

For example:

```
var Geometry={};
Geometry.units="inches";
Geometry.Point=function(x,y){
                this.x=x;
                this.y=y;
                this.add=function(){
                        return this.x+this.y;
                };
        };
var myPoint= new Geometry.Point(1,2);
```

There is nothing wrong with defining the Point constructor to be a property of a Geometry object, but because of the use of `new`, `this` is set to reference the new object that is being created and not the Geometry object, i.e. the call context. What this means is that that you cannot use `this` to reference the units property of the Geometry object. You can make it work, but only by putting the Geometry object inside a constructor and giving it a private variable that references it so that the Point constructor can access it.

This is not a practical issue, but it is important that the way that `this` is used in a constructor is completely understood.

As soon as you put `new` in front of a function call, `this` is no longer the call context.

Self or New?

The issue of using an object factory or an object constructor is a difficult topic. Most JavaScript programmers are introduced to using constructors as if it is the standard way of creating objects – it is. However, it has problems.

The first is that you have to remember to use `new` in front of a constructor call – and if you forget it then it doesn't work. You don't need to use `new` in front of an object factory call and the use of `self` produces early bound methods and properties.

Using a constructor brings with it some additional actions that make programming easier. These, in particular the constructor property and the prototype property, which are automatically set when you use `new` and a constructor, are the subject of the next chapter. However, they are not particularly useful and can introduce problems.

There is a compromise. You can use a constructor but use `self` rather than `this` by simply setting `self` to reference the same object as `this`.

For example:

```
var Point=function(x,y){
            var self=this;
            self.x=x;
            self.y=y;
            self.add=function(){
                    return self.x+self.y;
                };
        };
```

Notice that `self` is set to `this` as the first instruction. The only real difference is that in the definition of the add function the properties are early bound to the instance. If you want to use `this` in the creation of the object and `self` in method definitions you can. Indeed you can choose to use `self` or `this` in method definition depending on whether you want them early or late bound to the call context.

You can even test for the use of `new` in a call to the constructor by testing if `this` is the global object, usually `window`. If `this` is the global object the constructor has been called without using `new` and you simply call the constructor properly:

```
Point=function(x,y){
 if(this===window) return new Point(x,y);
    rest of constructor
```

If you can't assume what the global object is, set up a global variable to store a reference to it:

```
Global=this;
Point=function(x,y){
 if(this===Global) return new Point(x,y);
    rest of constructor
```

In ES2015 you can use the new.target property, which is set to the constructor when called with `new` and is undefined in all other function calls.

```
Point=function(x,y){
 if(!new.target) return new Point(x,y);
    rest of constructor
```

There are many variations in this basic theme. In general, however, the use of new in front of a constructor isn't a big problem.

Strict Mode

Note that in strict mode `this` will be set to undefined rather than the global object. The solution is to test for both situations.

Summary

- Object literals are fine for singleton objects, but even here there are advantages to the use of an object factory.

- An object factory creates an object complete with properties and methods and returns that object as its result.

- If the object factory declares the local variable `self` to reference the new object, then methods can use `self` to early bind to the object's properties.

- Any local variables or local functions defined within the object factory are accessible to the constructed object because of the operation of closure – thus providing private variables and methods to the object.

- JavaScript has the `new` operator, which if used in front of a function call makes it a constructor. A constructor automatically has `this` referencing a new empty object and automatically returns the object without the need for an explicit return.

- Notice that within a constructor `this` is not the call context but a new empty object.

- You can use `this` within a constructor in the same way as `self` in an object factory to refer to the new object and within methods to bind them to the object.

- You can add `self` to a constructor to get the benefit of both approaches.

- If you use `this` in a method definition then the method is late bound. If you use `self` in a method definition then the method is early bound.

- Finally you can make `new` optional in front of a constructor by a simple test and recall pattern, but this usually isn't necessary.

Chapter 10

The Prototype

The prototype is about the most mysterious part of JavaScript. Once you have mastered the call context and the constructor, it is the prototype that you have to turn to.

How does it work? How do you use it? What is it for?

The whole issue of the prototype object in JavaScript is a very contentious one – and don't expect to agree with everything I say in this introduction to the idea. What matters is that you understand completely what facilities are provided, why they were provided in the way that they are, and have some ideas how best to use them.

The prototype object is a very strange idea and making sense of it depends on seeing the bigger picture. The prototype object is intimately tied up with the idea and use of a constructor to create objects.

As we have already discovered in earlier chapters, there are other ways of creating objects than via a constructor and so this is not necessarily an essential part of JavaScript. You can choose to ignore constructors and prototypes, but most programmers make use of them to some extent.

The Prototype Delegation Principle

The actual prototype mechanism is very simple.

Every object has an internal [[prototype]] property. It is internal in the sense that you cannot access it directly. There are non-standard ways of accessing it, and in ES2015 there are standard ways, but in pre-ES2015 JavaScript it is simpler to regard it as inaccessible.

The question of how it gets set to reference another object is something that we will deal with later. For the moment what matters is that the [[prototype]] property is used to attempt to resolve any property references that the object does not support.

That is, if you try to use a property that hasn't been defined on an object then the system looks for it on the object that [[prototype]] references.

That is, the [[prototype]] references an object that will be used to delegate any properties or methods that the original object doesn't have.

This principle applies to all objects including any object referenced as a prototype. This means that if the prototype object doesn't have the property then its prototype object is searched and so on up the prototype chain.

The prototype chain ends when an object with a null [[prototype]] reference is encountered.

Thus every object has a prototype chain which consists of at least null.

Many ways of creating an object set the [[prototype]] property to reference the object Object.prototype and this has its [[prototype]] property set to null so automatically ending the chain.

So What is the Prototype Chain For?

The simple answer is that it provides a default set of behaviors for an object. If you set object A's prototype to be object B then, without any extra work, A automatically seems to have all of the properties of B.

Clearly if the same prototype object is used for a lot of other objects then this default behavior is obtained without having to duplicate all of the code. That is, one reason for using prototypes is that it is more efficient.

Another reason is that if a set of objects all have a single prototype object then updating that object updates all of the objects that use it as a prototype.

The temptation is to think of this as some sort of inheritance – but notice that this is not class-based inheritance and there is no suggestion that one object is a child or sub-object of another.

There is no type hierarchy in JavaScript. You might say that object A "inherits" the properties of object B but it is more accurate to think of object A delegating any access to properties it doesn't directly support. This is something we need to look more closely at in this and the next few chapters but the prototype mechanism is more like code reuse than inheritance.

Notice that this mechanism automatically shadows any prototype properties that the original object does implement. For example, if both A and its prototype B have property c then A.c accesses the property provided by A, and B's property is shadowed or overridden by A's.

Properties that are directly provided by an object are known as its "own" properties.

You can test to see if a property is directly provided using the hasOwnProperty function which is provided by the Object prototype. That is, any object that has Object in its prototype chain has access to a hasOwnProperty function – more of this later.

Setting [[prototype]]

The idea of the prototype chain and the way it provides additional properties for an object is fairly easy to understand. It is important that you keep this simplicity in sight while you get to grips with some of the messier details of how the prototype chain actually gets set up.

The first thing to say is that pre-ES5 things were subtle and involved the new operator and the general idea of a constructor. This is still the version that most JavaScript programmers know today and it is important - but it is easier to start with the latest ES5 features. These are supported by all modern browsers.

First two very simple and very basic settings of [[prototype]].

- The Object built-in constructor object has a prototype property that automatically references an object that provides default behavior for most JavaScript objects. For example, Object.prototype provides functions such as hasOwnProperty to other objects that have it in their prototype chain.

- When you create an object literal its [[prototype]] is set to reference the same object that Object.prototype references.

What this means is that all literal objects have the basic behavior provided by Object.prototype.

Now we come to the new ES5 facility.

The new:

```
Object.create(obj)
```

method can be used to create a new object with obj as its prototype - that is with its [[prototype]] property referencing obj.

Consider, for example:

```
var myProto={a:1,b:2,c:3};
var myObject= Object.create(myProto);
console.log(myObject.a);
```

This first creates a literal object which is going to be used as a prototype for another object. Next Object.create is used to create a new empty object but with its [[prototype]] referencing myProto.

Now when we try to use property a (or b or c) on the new object, clearly it isn't found as an own property, but the search of the prototype chain leads directly to myProto and it does have property a which is used as if it was a property of myObject.

Notice that the prototype chain in this example is:

```
myObject→ myProto→ Object.prototype→ null;
```

The literal object myProto has Object.prototype set as its prototype by default and Object.prototype has null as its prototype by default.

The only problem with Object.create is that it is not supported by older browsers. However, it is very easy to create a polyfill based on the original method of setting a prototype object - see later for more details.

Now we have a way of setting an object's prototype object we can explore some of its implications.

Object Prototype Interactions

The prototype object, and more generally the prototype chain, brings behavior to an object without you having to re-implement it.

In the normal course of things a prototype object would be used more than once as a prototype. If it is only used once you might as well use the prototype as the main object as there is no obvious advantage in delegating.

For example:

```
var myObject1 = Object.create(myProto);
var myObject2 = Object.create(myProto);
```

Now myObject1 and myObject2 have the same prototype object and hence the same values of a, b and c.

This raises the question of what happens if either of the objects tries to modify a property provided by the prototype?

The simple answer is that an object cannot modify a non-own property. For example, if you try:

```
var myObject1.a=10;
```

you will discover that myObject1.a is 10 and myObject2.a is still 1. When you try to store a value in a property the prototype chain is mostly ignored and an own property is created. From this moment on the own property is used and the prototype object's property is overridden.

Note: There is a subtle twist to this in that if the prototype's property is set as read only then the assignment is disallowed and a prototype property is created.

The object may not be able to modify the prototype object but any modifications to the prototype are immediately communicated to the object using it.

For example:

```
var myObject1 = Object.create(myProto);
var myObject2 = Object.create(myProto);
myProto.a=10;
```

results in both objects having a value of 10 for the a property - unless of course they have created an own property.

Using a prototype object to share data isn't often a good idea because as soon as the main object writes to a non-own property it is converted into an own property. This means you generally don't make any savings in storage when you supply data properties using a prototype unless that data is read only. A much better plan if you want to share data is to use a separate data object and set it as a property on each of the objects that want to use the data.

It is generally said that creating data properties on a prototype object is an "anti-pattern" but this mostly by comparison to what happens in class-based languages. If you have a reason for wanting to equip an object with a default set of data properties then using a prototype object is perfectly reasonable and safe.

The important point is that the prototype mechanism is dynamic.

Changes to the prototype object affect the properties of any object that is using it to supply those properties.

Improve Efficiency Using a Prototype

You can see that having a prototype as a sort of template for other objects might be useful but this is not the real reason for its introduction to JavaScript. The real reason is that it makes sharing methods between many objects much easier.

You get an efficiency gain when you supply a function as a property using a prototype.

Suppose you want some objects with a few properties and a method:

```
var myObject1 = {a: 1, b: 2, c: 3,
               myDisplay: function() {
                       console.log(this.a);
                   }
             };
var myObject2 = {a: 1, b: 2, c: 3,
               myDisplay: function() {
                       console.log(this.a);
                   }
             };
```

In this case myObject1 and myObject2 have their own separate Function objects referenced by their myDisplay property even though both functions do the same job. This isn't a theoretical problem but it is an avoidable duplication that gets worse with the number of objects creating identical Function objects. Notice that this situation is usually hidden within a constructor. The constructor creates the object and a new Function object each time it is used.

However, you can share the same Function object between as many other objects as you care to using the prototype mechanism.

For example:

```
var myProto = {a: 1, b: 2, c: 3,
            myDisplay: function() {
                    console.log(this.a);
                }
            };
```

Now the prototype has a method that displays its own property:

```
var myObject1 = Object.create(myProto);
var myObject2 = Object.create(myProto);
myObject1.myDisplay();
myObject2.myDisplay();
```

Now both objects display the value 1, but they both make use of the same Function object which is only referenced by the prototype object.

That is, there is one instance of the Function object referenced by the myDisplay property of myProto.

This is the main problem that the prototype mechanism was invented to solve.

In class-based languages methods that are defined in the class are not copied to every instance of the class - only the data is copied. That is, in class-based, object-oriented programming all instances share the common code in the methods defined in the class, but they each have their own data.

The prototype mechanism allows you to share a single implementation of methods between a set of objects.

That is, the prototype mechanism was introduced into JavaScript to mimic the method sharing implemented by class-based languages.

Notice that the prototype mechanism isn't the only way to share methods between objects, you can simply define a Function object that makes use of this and assign the Function to multiple object properties as described in earlier chapters. See Shared Instance Methods in Chapter 8.

For example:

```
var myProto = {a: 1, b: 2, c: 3,};
var myDisplay = function() {
                console.log(this.a);
              };

var myObject1 = Object.create(myProto);
myObject1.myDisplay=myDisplay;

var myObject2 = Object.create(myProto);
myObject2.myDisplay=myDisplay;

myObject1.myDisplay();
myObject2.myDisplay();
```

As before myObject1 and myObject2 now share a single instance of the Function object referenced by myDisplay. Notice that apart from being slightly harder to set up it behaves much like a prototype method. If either myObject1 or myObject2 redefine myDisplay then the redefined version takes priority over the initial Function object.

That is, you don't really need the prototype property to share methods and it could have been left out of JavaScript in favor of manually creating Function objects to share.

The main advantage of the prototype mechanism is that it adds a set of methods and properties to the object in one neat package.

All you have to do is set up the prototype object with all the shared methods and then set it as the prototype for all the objects you create.

There is also the fact that you can use multiple prototype objects via the prototype chain.

To a programmer familiar with class-based objects this looks a lot like either inheritance or multiple inheritance depending on whether or not the prototype objects form a natural hierarchy - i.e. does each one "extend" in some sense the previous one.

There is one final subtle point concerning the use of this.

In the definition of the prototype:

```
var myProto = {a: 1, b: 2, c: 3,
              myDisplay: function() {
                      console.log(this.a);
                  }
              };
```

we have a reference to this.a.

What does this reference?

The good news is that it follows the usual logic. The `this` is set to the call context.

So if you call:

```
myProto.myDisplay();
```

`this` is set to myProto.

If you call:

```
myObject1.myDisplay();
```

`this` is set to myObject1 but myDisplay isn't an own property and so it is resolved by the prototype chain, i.e. myProto supplies the function. The `this` still references myObject1 but when myDisplay tries to access myObject1.a it can't find it and so the prototype chain is used again and `this` resolves to the a supplied by myProto.

Now let's shadow the a property by creating an own property:

```
var myObject1 = Object.create(myProto);
var myObject2 = Object.create(myProto);

myObject1.a=10;
myObject1.myDisplay();
myObject2.myDisplay();
```

The first call to myDisplay has `this` set to myObject1 and myDisplay is supplied by myProto but myObject1.a exists as an own property so it displays 10. The second call works in the same way but myObject2.a isn't an own object and so is supplied by myProto.

The rule is that `this` is set to the calling context of the object and any methods supplied by the prototype object are executed in this context.

Binding and the Prototype

It is important to notice, from the previous discussion, that the correct functioning of the prototype chain depends on late binding. If a method is supplied to an object via the prototype chain then it will only work with properties of the method if the method is using `this` to late bind.

For example suppose we had written:

```
var myProto = {a: 1, b: 2, c: 3,
            myDisplay: function() {
                    console.log(myProto.a);
                }
        };
```

You can replace `this` with any of the early bound forms we looked at in previous chapters i.e. using bind say.

Then when it is called as:

```
myObject1.myDisplay();
```

this would be set to myObject1 and this would be true for every object in the prototype chain. However, as the method is early bound to myProto, it will only display the value of myProto.a which is fine as long as myObject1 is using the property a via the prototype chain. As soon as myObject1 defines its own property a everything stops working as expected as myDisplay displays myProto.a and not myObject1.a.

The problem with this sort of early binding error is that it often doesn't show until later in the development of the program when the object acquires its own versions of prototype chain properties.

If you are going to use an object in the prototype chain then make sure that all of the methods are late bound using this.

A Simple Example

If your object is a singleton, there will only ever be a single instance of the object, so you often don't need to worry about prototypes. In a typical JavaScript program most of the objects are singletons and in this case there is little to be gained from using a prototype. The main exception to this tendency towards singletons are objects designed to store and process data.

In this case there is often a lot to be gained from using a prototype.

For example, a typical 2D point object might be defined as:

```
var point1 = {x:0, y:0,
              setxy:function(x, y) {
                      this.x = x;
                      this.y = y;
                  }
             };
```

and a typical use might be:

```
point1.setxy(10,200);
console.log(point1.x,point1.y);
```

If you want a second point you would define the whole thing over again - probably using an object factory or a constructor rather than manually:

```
var point2 = {x:0, y:0,
              setxy:function(x, y) {
                      this.x = x;
                      this.y = y;
                  }
             };
```

If you wanted 5000 point objects then having the setxy function defined as 5000 identical Function objects, one for each instance, is a little wasteful.

A better solution is to set up a prototype object with the methods that a point object needs:

```
var pointMethods={
                setxy:function(x, y) {
                        this.x = x;
                        this.y = y;
                }
        };
```

You could include the initial data variables x, y if you want to, or they could be created on the instances as own properties - it doesn't make a great deal of difference.

Now you can create two point objects very easily:

```
var point1 = Object.create(pointMethods);
var point2 = Object.create(pointMethods);
point1.setxy(10,200);
console.log(point1.x,point1.y);
```

Notice that in this case the call to setxy creates the two own properties x and y for us. In general it is better to create any variables either as own variables or as part of the prototype rather than just rely on a method to do the job as a side effect. The general consensus is that data properties should always belong to the instance.

If you are creating a data object then using the prototype is the easiest way of sharing methods between instances.

The Extended Role of the Constructor

If you have followed the idea of the prototype object and the way it provides a delegation mechanism for any properties that are not defined on an object, be reassured that it really is this simple. However, there is a slightly more complicated way of setting an object's [[prototype]] property that was designed early in the life of JavaScript to provide something that looked like a class-based type and inheritance mechanism.

Recall that a constructor is just a function that is called with the new operator and returns an object.

The idea is that the constructor is a special sort of object factory.

JavaScript takes this idea one step further and for some it is a step too far.

The idea is that a constructor can be used to create many instances of an object. This is a bit like the way in class-oriented languages a class can be used to create many instances of an object.

So a constructor can play the same role as class in that it weakly defines a "type" of object.

Put simply, the assumption is that if a constructor creates lots of instances of an object then they can be regarded as being of the same type. In this sense the constructor plays the role of a class and it defines an object type.

This isn't unreasonable in the sense that any object that a constructor creates has the same set of properties as all the others it creates and what properties an object has defines its type.

If a constructor is so important in the life of an object, why not allow it to play a role in the setting of an object's prototype chain. This is again part of thinking of the constructor as if it defined a class - complete with a hierarchy of classes it inherits from.

The constructor prototype mechanism is:

- Every function object has a prototype property which is by default set to a null object {}.
- This is not the internal [[prototype]] property and it doesn't reference the function's prototype chain.
- When a function is called with the new operator, i.e. as a constructor, the object it creates has its internal [[prototype]] property set to the constructor's prototype property.
- That is, the function's prototype property sets the prototype chain of the objects it creates.

This makes sense if you want to regard the constructor as playing the same role as a class.

Every object that the constructor produces has the same set of properties and the same prototype chain.

As an example of this approach to setting the prototype we can re-implement the 2D point object.

We can leave the definition of the point prototype object as it was:

```
var pointMethods={
                setxy:function(x, y) {
                        this.x = x;
                        this.y = y;
                }
        };
```

Now we are going to use a constructor to create a point object:

```
function Point(){
   this.x=0;
   this.y=0;
}
Point.prototype=pointMethods;
```

Notice that now we have set the constructor's prototype property to the pointMethods object.

It is more idiomatic to write the above as:

```
Point.prototype.setxy= function(x, y) {
                        this.x = x;
                        this.y = y;
                      }
```

There is no real difference but it saves inventing a name for the prototype object. Notice that you are adding properties to the default object {} that the prototype property is initially set to.

Again it is important to stress that pointMethods is not the constructor function's prototype which is a common misconception. It will be used as the prototype object for any objects the constructor creates.

For example:

```
var point1 = new Point();
var point2 = new Point();
point1.setxy(10,200);
console.log(point1.x);
console.log(point1.y);
```

Now both point1 and point2 have pointMethods as their prototype.

Object Factories and Prototype

If you want to use an object factory rather than a constructor you can still arrange it to set the object's prototype without requiring the explicit use of new.

All you have to do is make use of the new operator within the factory to create a dummy function, set its prototype property, and then use it to create an empty object with its prototype chain set.

For example, a factory method for the point object is:

```
function Point(){
 var F=function(){};
 F.prototype=pointMethods;
 var Pointobj=new F();
 obj.x=0;
 obj.y=0;
 return obj;
}
```

This may look a little strange but it is perfectly good. F is a function object that does nothing. Its prototype property is set to pointMethods and then the new operator is used to call it as a constructor. It constructs an empty object i.e. {} but with its [[prototype]] set to pointMethods.

After this the factory method builds the object in the usual way and can be called without needing a new:

```
var point1 = Point();
var point2 = Point();
point1.setxy(10,200);
console.log(point1.x,point1.y);
```

You should be able to see that this also provide a polyfill for the Object.create method:

```
function ObjectCreate(proto){
  var F=function(){};
  F.prototype=proto;
  return new F();
}
```

This simply returns an empty object with its prototype set to proto, just like the Object.create(proto) method.

There are many variations on this basic theme. For example we can make use of the fact that every Function object has a prototype property, not just constructors, to make our factory object look more like a constructor:

```
function Point(){
 var F=function(){};
 F.prototype=Point.prototype;
 var obj=new F();
 obj.x=0;
 obj.y=0;
 return obj;
}
Point.prototype=pointMethods;
```

Notice that now the prototype of the objects created is set by the Point.prototype property.

The Prototype is an Object Not a Class

One of the biggest problems in adapting to the idea of a prototype chain is that it looks a lot like a class hierarchy and it isn't.

The prototype object is just that – an object.

Obvious, you may say, but consider the following.

Suppose you have a constructor Point, which creates very simple 2D Point objects:

```
function Point(x,y){
  this.x=x;
  this.y=y;
}
```

You would use this to create as many instances of the Point object as you require:

```
var p1=new Point(0,0);
var p2=new Point(1,1);
```

and so on...

Now consider that you want to create a new 3D Point constructor and have it "inherit" from Point.

The question is, which instance of Point should be its prototype object?

For example:

```
function Point3D(x,y,z){
  this.z=z
}
Point3D.prototype=p1;
```

constructs instances of Point3D where the prototype is p1 but:

```
function Point3D(x,y,z){
this.z=z
}
Point3D.prototype=p2;
```

constructs instances of Point3D where the prototype is p2.

These are different and there is no way that you can create Point3D so that it "inherits" from some generic Point2D "class". The difference is important because if changes occur to p1 then the prototype of the first is changed but not the prototype of the second.

This is very different from class-based inheritance where at runtime there are no changes to the class and the inheritance is static.

Using prototype objects means that "inheritance" is tied to an object which might be regarded as an instance of a "class" but it can dynamically change at runtime.

So what instance should you use as the prototype?

Ideally the prototype should be a singleton and this implies that an object literal is a good choice.

If you do have a constructor for an object that you want to use as a prototype, then the best idea is to create a new instance specifically for the job.

For example:

```
function Point3D(x,y,z){
  this.z=z
}
Point3D.prototype=new Point2(0,0);
```

This decouples your new constructor from any other instances but notice that any changes to the prototype object are still passed on to the instances. For example:

```
Point3D.prototype.x=10:
```

changes the initial value of x in all of the Point3D objects created that haven't their own x property.

There are many traps waiting for the ambitious user of the prototype mechanism that are related to it being a prototype object and not a class.

Many programmers find it irritating that the prototype is set outside of the constructor. In an attempt to tidy things up you could try to define it within the constructor to make it clear that this is a method intended for Point as in:

```
function Point() {
  Point.prototype.setxy = function (x, y) {
                            this.x = x;
                            this.y = y;
                          };
  this.x = 0;
  this.y = 0;
}
```

but notice that this creates a new Function object each time the constructor is called, which will work, but if you create 10,000 Point objects might be inefficient. In fact you might as well just define setxy as an instance method because it creates the same number of Function objects.

Prototype Editing

The final problem is that new objects don't just acquire a prototype object they really do acquire a prototype chain.

If you create objectA with null prototype and objectB with prototype objectA then if you next create objectC with prototype objectB then it also gets objectA as part of the chain.

Why is this important?

Suppose we now want objectC to have just objectB as its prototype and not objectA. There is no way to do this without changing the prototype of objectB and this also changes the prototype chain of any other objects that have objectB as their prototype.

The fact that it is a good idea to use singletons as prototype objects, and the way prototype chains work, means editing or modify a prototype is a difficult and dangerous thing to do.

You can do it, however, as there are getPrototypeOf and setPrototypeOf methods of the ES2015 Object constructor.

For example, if we assume that the prototype chain of objectC is:

`objectC→ objectB→ objectA`

then:

`Object.getPrototypeOf(objectC);`

returns ObjectB.

Similarly:

`Object.setPrototypeOf(objectB,null);`

sets the prototype of objectB to null. Notice that this changes the prototype chain of objectC and any object that has objectB in its prototype chain.

That is, changing the prototype of any object has effects on any other object that has it anywhere in its prototype chain.

Changing prototypes is not a local operation and as such is very difficult to keep under control.

If you have to edit the prototype chain then the only safe thing to do is to insert a brand new object at the start.

For example assuming that the prototype chain is:

`objectC→ objectB→ objectA`

you can add objectD to the chain using:

```
var objectD=new ObjectD();
Object.setPrototypeOf(Object.getPrototypeOf(objectC);
Object.setPrototypeOf(objectC,objectD);
```

This produces a prototype chain with objectD at the start:

`objectC→ objectD→ objectB→ objectA`

Notice that if objectD already existed then in adding it to the prototype chain you would have changed its prototype chain and hence any prototype chains that depended on it.

Adding a new instance to the start of a prototype chain is the only safe prototype edit.

Prototypes of Built-in Objects

One of the things that can be confusing is that the constructors of the built-in objects also have prototype properties which are used to set the prototype of any instances you create.

Again it is important to remember that it is the internal [[prototype]] property that determines an object's prototype chain and the constructor's prototype property is used to set this internal property when an instance is created.

Each of the built-in objects has a unique standard prototype chain for its instances.

Simple object instances have a single object prototype chain:

```
object→ object prototype→ null
```

All of the other special object instances - boolean, number, string, array, date and so on have an additional prototype object before object prototype. For example:

```
string→ string prototype→ object prototype→ null
```

Some of the prototypes earlier in the chain override methods provided by the object prototype. For example, the object prototype provides both toString and toValue and these are both overridden by the string prototype.

You can modify the prototype object used by the constructors if you want to.

For example:

```
Object.prototype
```

is a reference to the object prototype object. So if you want to add a property to the prototype object used by every object in JavaScript you would write:

```
Object.prototype.myprop=function(){
                  console.log("Object Proto");
              };
```

Following this you can write:

```
var obj={};
obj.myprop;
```

and the prototype chain will provide the function.

As the object prototype is the final object in all of the prototype chains you can also write:

```
var fun=function(){};
fun.myprop;
```

or:

```
var array=[1,2,3];
array.myprop;
```

If you only want to add or modify a property of a specific object type then you can change just its specific prototype. For example to change the function prototype you would use:

```
Function.prototype.myprop=function(){console.log("Function Proto");}
```

Now when you try:

```
var fun=function(){};
fun.myprop;
```

you will see Function Proto but when you try:

```
var obj={};
obj.myprop;
```

you will still see Object Proto.

Modifying and adding to the built-in objects' instance prototypes is a way of modifying and extending the behavior of every instance.

This is generally considered to be a bad idea and you are warned not to do it by everyone. Part of the reason is that a well-known library called Prototype got into all sorts of trouble by adding features to the built-in object, but this was mainly because it caused interoperability problems with other libraries. There is nothing intrinsically wrong with adding functionality to the built-in instance object prototypes as long as you can ensure there will be no clashes and it is made clear what is happening.

Class in ES2015

ES2015 introduced some additional syntax which makes JavaScript's combination of constructor and prototype look a lot like class-based inheritance. It is important to realize that these changes are syntactic and make use of the same mechanisms we have been looking at.

In other words ES2015 my have a class statement but it still doesn't have classes.

Let us have a look at the new syntax and see how it relates to the constructor and the prototype.

You can declare a class using:

```
class Point {
    constructor(x, y) {
      this.x = x;
      this.y = y;
      this.setxy = function (x, y) {
                    this.x = x;
                    this.y = y;
                };
    }
}
```

which can be regarded as a shorthand for:

```
function Point(x, y) {
  this.x = x;
  this.y = y;
  this.setxy = function (x, y) {
                  this.x = x;
                  this.y = y;
               };
}
```

The important differences are that the class statement is not hoisted and so has to occur before the first use of the constructor, and you have to call the Point function using new. Also the body of the class statement is executed in strict mode. If you don't provide a constructor then a default function is created which returns the empty object {}.

As well as class declarations there are also class expressions:

```
var Point=class{
             constructor(x, y) { …
```

The only difference is that class expressions allow a class to be redefined, whereas a class statement throws an exception if you try to redefine it.

Prototype Methods

Notice that each object constructed using Point has its own x, y and setxy function. Unless Point is going to be a singleton it doesn't make good sense to define a new setxy function for every instance. Any functions which are defined in the class body but outside of the constructor are added to the prototype object and this is a convenient way of sharing code between all of the instances.

For example, if we move setxy outside of the constructor:

```
class Point {
   constructor(x, y) {
     this.x = x;
     this.y = y;
   };
   setxy(x, y) {
     this.x = x;
     this.y = y;
   };
}
```

then it is added to the prototype object.

In this case the class definition is equivalent to:

```
function Point(x, y) {
  this.x = x;
  this.y = y;
}
Point.prototype.setxy = function (x, y) {
                          this.x = x;
                          this.y = y;
                        };
```

Methods defined in the constructor are own methods and those defined in the class body are prototype methods.

You can only define methods and not data properties as it is considered bad practice to place data into the prototype. If you want to add data to the prototype then you have to return to the original way of doing it, i.e.:

```
Point.prototype.z=0;
```

You can do this because the class creates a constructor function called Point which has a prototype property just like all Function objects.

The class syntax makes it so easy to define prototype methods that it is a standard way of defining methods even for a singleton.

The standard pattern is to always define methods in the class body and data in the constructor.

Another common pattern is to use get and set in the class to allow access to data properties in the constructor:

```
class Point {
  constructor(x, y) {
    this.x = x;
    this.y = y;
  }
  get x() {
    return this.x;
  }
  set x(value) {
    this.x = value;
  }
}
```

In this case x and y are instance variables i.e. each instance gets its own x and y, but the get and set functions are shared by all the instances via the prototype object.

Static Methods

You can also define static methods which are methods of the constructor. That is, a static method is a method of the Function Point and not of any object constructed by Point. Static methods don't have access to the properties of the instances and they are generally called so that this is set to the constructor.

For example:

```
class Point {
   constructor(x, y) {
      this.x = x;
      this.y = y;
   }
   static display(x) {
     alert(x);
   }
}
```

This adds the function display to the Point Function object.

To use it you would write:

```
Point.display(10);
```

As display is a method of Point it has no access to x and y as defined in the constructor and realized in any of its instances. When display is called this is set to Point and in principle it could have access to any data properties defined on Point but there is no way to define such properties using static.

You can, however, create properties on the Point Function object in the traditional way:

```
Point.z=10;
```

and then you could write:

```
class Point {
   constructor(x, y) {
      this.x = x;
      this.y = y;
   }
   static display() {
     alert(this.z);
   }
}
```

You need to be very clear that z is a property of Point and not of any instances that Point creates.

The main use of static methods are to provide utility functions that work with the instances of the class.

The standard example is a compare function:

```
class Point {
    constructor(x, y) {
        this.x = x;
        this.y = y;
    }
    static equal(p1,p2) {
        return p1.x==p2.x && p1.y==p2.y;
    }
}
```

which could be used as:

```
Point.equal(point1,point2);
```

where point1 and point2 are instances.

Notice that there is no special relationship between the static method and what is passed to it e.g. p1 and p2 could be anything not just instances of Point.

Private Methods and Data

What about private methods and variables?

Although there is no provision for private entities in the class syntax i.e. no private keyword, you can still declare variables in the constructor and rely on closure to make them available to instance methods.

For example:

```
class Point {
    constructor(x, y) {
        this.x = x;
        this.y = y;
        var z = 100;
        this.display = function () {
                        alert(z);
                      };
    }
}
```

The private variable z is available to the instance method display because of the closure. Notice that private variables are not available to prototype methods as these do not have access to the closure.

So to summarize:

There are three types of method you can define using class:

- ◆ An instance method is defined in the constructor and each instance gets its own Function object.

- ◆ A prototype method is defined in the body of the class and each instance uses the same Function object via the prototype.

- ◆ A static method is defined in the body of the class using the keyword static and this is a property of the class Function.

There is also a fourth type of method which is not supported by the class syntax but still works:

- ◆ A private method is defined in the constructor as a local variable and shared between all of the instance methods. It is not available to any prototype methods.

Extends – Inheritance the Class Way ES2015

There are a number of ways of implementing inheritance in JavaScript as well as simply using the prototype chain. The class syntax formalizes one particularly attractive way of inheriting methods and properties from existing objects in the extends keyword.

The idea is that you can use a class or a constructor as if it was a more traditional class and inherit it as the basis for building an extended class.

For example suppose we start off with a simple Point class:

```
class Point {
    constructor(x, y) {
        this.x = x;
        this.y = y;
    }
}
```

we could use this to create a 3D Point class by adding a z coordinate. To do this we can create the new class Point3D that extends Point:

```
class Point3D extends Point{
    constructor(x,y,z){
        super(x,y);
        this.z=z;
    }
}
```

There are two new keywords being used – extends and super.

The extends keyword makes Point the base for the new class. The super keyword calls the base class constructor and sets `this` to reference the new instance. Obviously you cannot use `this` until after you have called super.

That is, the above is equivalent to:

```
function Point3D(x,y,z){
 this=new Point(x,y);
 this.z=z;
}
```

You can see that where normally `this` is set to {} which is then expanded by having properties added to it, here `this` is set to an instance of Point which likewise has properties added to it. You could say that the null object {} is the default base class but by calling super you use an instance of an existing class.

Notice that there are two ways that the new object inherits from the base object.

First it inherits all of the instance properties via the use of the original constructor and these are inherited as instance properties.

Second it inherits via the prototype chain all of the prototype properties i.e. methods.

Of course you can make use of the prototype object of the base instance to define new prototype methods as well as static methods. Notice that static methods are not inherited by the constructor.

There is a small subtlety here.

The prototype of the new object isn't just set to the prototype of the existing class. If is was, then any changes that the new class made to the prototype would change the prototype of the original class. What happens is that the prototype is set to a new empty object which has its prototype set to the prototype of the original object.

That is the new constructor is more like:

```
function Point3D(x,y,z){
   this=new Point(x,y);
   this.z=z;
}
Point3D.prototype=Object.create(Point2D.prototype);
```

This clearly allows the Point3D constructor to add properties to the new null object prototype without modifying the prototype belonging to Point2D and yet it still has access to all of its prototype properties.

Given the problems with using the Prototype chain as a stand in for class-based inheritance, this is a much better way of doing the job but notice that each instance of the subtype gets its own instance of the base type. This doesn't make any difference to efficiency as long as all of the base type's methods are prototype methods which is of course the best practice you should be following anyway.

An Example

Consider the following class:

```
class Point2D {
    constructor(x, y) {
        this.x = x;
        this.y = y;
    }
    setxy(x, y) {
        this.x = x;
        this.y = y;
    }
    display() {
        console.log(this.x + "," + this.y);
    }
}
```

Notice that the data is in the constructor and hence implemented as instance properties, but the methods are in the class body, and hence implemented as prototype properties.

The ES5 version of this class is:

```
function Point2D(x, y) {
    this.x = x;
    this.y = y;
}
Point2D.prototype.setxy=function(x, y) {
                        this.x = x;
                        this.y = y;
                }
Point2D.prototype.display=function() {
                        console.log(this.x + "," + this.y);
                }
```

Now we can derive a Point3D class by inheriting from the Point2D class:

```
class Point3D extends Point2D {
    constructor(x, y, z) {
        super(x, y);
        this.z = z;
    }
    display() {
        console.log(this.x + "," + this.y + "," + this.z);
    }
}
```

Notice that Point2D supplies the data x and y as instance properties and the display method via the prototype. Also notice that Point3D overrides the inherited version of display to one that works with x, y and z.

The ES2015 version of this class is:

```
function Point3D(x, y, z) {
  var this=Point2D(x, y);
  this.z = z;
}
Point3D.prototype=Object.create(Point2D.prototype);
Point3D.prototype.display=function() {
                         console.log(this.x + ","
                             + this.y + "," + this.z);
                         }
```

Now you can create Point2D objects and Point3D objects and they will use the correct version of display:

```
var point1 = new Point2D(1, 2);
var point2 = new Point3D(1, 2, 3);
point1.display();
point3.display();
```

The first display shows x and y and the second shows x, y and z.

Code Reuse

Understanding and using the prototype principle is difficult because it really is only part of the solution to the code reuse problem.

The ES2015 class syntax does formalize what is probably the best way to organize code reuse in JavaScript – even if you don't make use of the class syntax.

It involves using the prototype chain and the constructor:

- ◆ use a constructor for any object you want to create
- ◆ make all methods prototype methods
- ◆ make all data instance properties
- ◆ implement inheritance by calling the constructor of the "class" you want to inherit from as the initial object that the constructor creates.

These are exactly the same steps that the class/extend syntax uses.

Using Prototypes

You can think of the prototype mechanisms as providing some sort of inheritance - but it certainly doesn't bring with it any of the workings of an inheritance hierarchy.

The main reason is that the prototype mechanism is based on instances rather than a class hierarchy.

It is a much simpler and much more direct mechanism to make code sharing possible.

If you have a single object then there isn't much practical advantage in designing a prototype object for it. On the other hand having a prototype object with all of the methods that the object is using does provide an organization. The object then has just the instance variables and the methods are all provided by the prototype. If things change and you need a second object, or more objects, then the prototype provides an easy solution.

You can go a step further and construct a chain of prototype objects, each one adding more specialized functionality. This is as close as JavaScript gets to an equivalent of an inheritance hierarchy, but notice it has none of the implications of a type hierarchy. In JavaScript an object is basically a bag of properties and a variable can reference any object.

The bottom line is that there may be situations in which a prototype hierarchy makes sense, but it isn't the default architecture as it is in a class-based language.

There is an argument for regarding prototype objects as method libraries for other objects which offer data storage.

As to the class syntax introduced in ES2015, it adds nothing fundamentally new but it formalizes the split between constructor and prototype based inheritance.

That is, the constructor is used to implement instance properties, and the prototype is used to implement prototype methods.

This is a good way to organize things but not the only way.

Summary

- All objects have an internal [[prototype]] property that references a prototype object. The prototype object also has a [[prototype]] property that references a prototype object and so on forming a prototype chain. The chain ends with a null object.

- When a property cannot be found on an object, the system searches the prototype chain to find it. The first prototype object to support the property is used.

- A property provided directly by the object is called an own property.

- You can set the prototype of an object using Object.create(*prototype*) which returns an empty object with [[prototype]] referencing the given *prototype* object.

- The prototype chain is live in the sense you can update it at any time.

- If an object tries to assign to a property provided by the prototype chain then it immediately creates an own property which shadows the prototype property. This is how you can override prototype provided methods.

- A constructor, a function called with new, creates an object and sets that object's [[prototype]] property to its prototype property.

- The prototype chain can be used to provide methods to a set of objects without incurring the overhead of duplicating the methods. It also means that a change to a prototype object immediately affects all of the objects that make use of it.

- The built-in objects, e.g. array, string and so on, all have their own constructors which have prototype properties which set the prototype chain. You can modify these prototype objects, but many regard this as a bad idea.

- Editing the prototype chain is difficult because it isn't a local operation. The only reasonably safe prototype chain edit is to add a new object to the start of the chain.

- The ES2015 class, private, extends and super keywords can be used to make constructors and prototypes look more like classes.

- The prototype chain can be used to implement something that resembles inheritance.

- Objects in JavaScript are just dynamic bags of properties and the prototype object can act as a library of properties and methods for other objects.

Chapter 11

Inheritance and Type

In this chapter we take a very general look at the prevailing dominant programming methodology – class-based, strongly-typed languages. This isn't particularly about JavaScript because, of course, it isn't class-based and it is hardly typed at all.

The belief that the only way to create a large program is to work with a strongly-typed language is strongly held and by people who have earned the right to be taken seriously. However, there are problems with the approach and there is hardly any evidence that it is better than the alternatives. What evidence there is, is weak and doesn't investigate how much harder strong typing makes programming.

In short, the attitude that there is only one way to program is an opinion.

Even so it is held with such conviction that it has caused people to invent improvements on JavaScript such as TypeScript, and has resulted in JavaScript being modified to move towards the middle ground of being more class-based and finding substitutes for type.

Most of these attempts, especially the ad-hoc additions to JavaScript, have had the reverse effect of making things more difficult. In the next chapter we review some of the, mostly failed, ways that type and class have been re-introduced to JavaScript.

In this chapter we look at the ideas of class and type to investigate what JavaScript lacks because it doesn't have them and understand what it gains.

What is more difficult to do in JavaScript than in a typed language? Are there things that are easy in JavaScript because it isn't strongly-typed?

The whole subject of type in programming is huge and this chapter cannot cover all aspects of the topic. It can't even cover all of the implications and consequences of adopting type. You do have to make up your own mind about type rather than just accept strong typing as being the overwhelming programming paradigm in use today.

You are unlikely to agree with everything in this chapter, but consider it food for thought.

Three Types Of Type

Even before we get started it is important to realize that there are a number of meanings to the word "type" in programming.

The most common usage of the word means primitive data type and after this it refers to the "class" that defines an object.

Exactly what these two meanings of type are all about will be explained in more detail later. For the moment it is assumed that you have a rough idea what a primitive type is e.g. an int or a string say, and you have an idea what a class-based type is i.e. an instance of a class.

There is also a third meaning which corresponds to algebraic data type and this is a much deeper almost philosophical idea, the Howard Curry correspondence, that really doesn't have much to do with JavaScript or the class-based languages that most of us know.

Such ideas of data typing are part of pure functional programming as found in languages such as Haskell and there is a lot to say about them, but it isn't really mainstream in the sense of languages like JavaScript, Java, C++, etc. It makes sense to concentrate on a comparison of JavaScript and class-based languages rather than functional languages.

For the rest of this chapter type will be taken to mean either primitive data type or class-based type.

What Is Type For?

So what is type for?

Put simply, type tells you the operations that you can perform.

By declaring the type of an object you specify exactly what operations you can use and what methods you can call.

If you know that x is of type integer then you know that it is fine to perform x+3 and not only do you know it, but the compiler knows it as well. This allows the compiler to detect incorrect code and flag type errors at compile time - thus saving you from the embarrassment of a runtime error.

This is already a problem for JavaScript because in most cases it doesn't have a compile time. In JavaScript you could argue that runtime errors are the only possibility, but we can equate the compile step in languages such as Java with the editing step in JavaScript.

In the case of an object, knowing its type defines precisely what methods and properties it has. This allows the compiler to check that you aren't calling any methods or accessing any properties that the object doesn't support. Again it is saving you from the embarrassment of a runtime error.

This is a worthwhile idea but it also limits what you can do and forces you to introduce other mechanisms to get over the restrictions strong typing brings with it.

There is a trade off in what strong typing gives you and what it stops you doing.

When you accept strong typing and type checking, it becomes possible to find some types of error but these errors are fairly easy to find in other ways. After all you simply have to check that every operation on an object is legal. If this can be done at compile time then it can be done by reading the code – i.e. by static analysis.

This approach is often referred to as "type inference" but you could just as well call it "property checking".

If you do adopt strong typing what you lose in return are ways of working that are type free - for example generic algorithms - and most languages have to invent complicated ways of restoring these features e.g. generics, covariance, contravariance and so on.

In short, type checking finds errors that are mostly easy to find without it.

Because of languages such as Java, C#, C++ and so on, most programmers are taught that strong typing is nothing but good and in fact you can't develop quality software without it.

This point of view is far from proven, most studies have proved that strong typing brings small advantages and they ignore its many disadvantages. To have a balanced view you really need to see both sides of the coin. You need to see clearly what typing is for, and what it does for you, and what it stops you doing.

So we have two general meanings of the word type - primitive type and class-based type.

The first and most basic relates to primitive data type.

In many ways this is the least important meaning of type - but it leads on to the more sophisticated class-based data type.

Primitive Data Typing

Primitive data typing is so ingrained in most approaches to programming that it is difficult to see it afresh and consider its implications.

In JavaScript the attempt to get away from primitive data typing is a bit of a half finished mess which confuses many beginners and experienced programmers alike. It gives rise to the seemingly complicated set of data coercion rules that cause data of apparently irreconcilable different types to be automatically converted without the programmer's intervention.

For the moment try to ignore the imperfect way JavaScript deals with primitive type and concentrate on the principles.

The idea of primitive type is deeply embedded in nearly all programming languages and hence in the minds of most programmers. As a result the alternative position of trying to eradicate all primitive data types which is outlined below is usually met with a great deal of resistance.

Try to keep an open mind.

Historically this is where the whole idea of type originated because it was necessary to make the distinction between different types of data for reasons of efficiency and how they were represented at the bit level. As time has passed it has become less and less necessary to worry how data is actually stored, and computer languages have become increasingly abstract and removed from the constraints of hardware.

The point is that what we program should never depend on the low level detail of how the bits are stored - and as long as it does we are still in a primitive state of development.

The object of any high level language is to abstract away from the reality of hardware, bits and representations.

In an ideal world we wouldn't worry too much about low level concepts such as primitive data type because the language would take care of everything. Instead of worrying about the format that data is stored in you would concentrate on the operations that you apply to data.

This is a difficult idea to take on board because as programmers we know for a fact that a number is stored in one way and a string, say, is stored in another. In fact we even know that numbers - integers and floats - are stored in different ways.

These differences are so ingrained that it is difficult to see or agree with the assertion that this isn't necessary.

You may say - yes it is - because numbers are different from text and you need integers and reals and so on.

No you don't - you simply need operators that do the right job. Most ideas of primitive type are in fact the result of not defining operators in the correct way.

For example, the addition operator would expect to work with two numbers and the concatenation operator would expect to work with two strings. The form that the data is stored in shouldn't matter and in this sense 123 and "123" are numbers - a string that happens to represent a number is a number. In the same way the concatenation operator would treat any number as a string.

What if you try to add a string that doesn't represent a valid number?

You get an error - what else could possibly happen - but throwing an error when the string does represent a valid number is ignoring what is in front of you.

The internal representation of data should be irrelevant to the operation of a high level program.

This is how humans work with data and we are the pinnacle of sophistication and abstraction. If I ask you to add 1 to 2 you don't worry about the data representation - are they strings or integers or what? Clearly they are valid numbers so you get on and add them.

Similarly, if I ask you to concatenate 123 at the end of the "some string of words" then you just do it. Again you don't worry about the difference between text and numeric values.

It is not the data representation that matters but the operation.

From the point of view of sophisticated abstraction the complete beginner is close to the ideal when they complain that there really is no difference between 123 and "123".

- There really is no difference between 123 and "123" that the language system cannot be left to sort out.

and

- In this data type-less world it really is the operator that determines the form of the operation and not the data.

In an ideal world, for example, the addition operator and the concatenation operator would be distinct + and & say. When you write a+b this would be addition irrespective of what a and b are, and a&b would be text concatenation. Notice that a+b might throw an error if either a or b could not be interpreted or coerced to a number - this is reasonable.

Throwing an error in any other case is being too picky and yet many programmers believe that this is what should happen "you can't use a string as if it was a number".

Sadly in JavaScript things aren't so pure.

The two operators are both represented by + and what a+b means depends on the primitive types of a and b - this is not good.

What about the logical distinctions between integers and reals?

Surely this is a data type distinction that is founded in mathematics?

Mathematically there are integers, rationals and irrationals. Some math programming languages have all three types, but in most cases all we need is one type of number that can be either an integer or a decimal rational as the need arises.

Integer and rational operations need only to be built into the operators not the data.

This is how things work in JavaScript.

There is a single numeric data type and how this is treated - integer or real - depends on the operator you use.

You also don't need notions of int32 or int64 to work with integer arithmetic - you simply need an integer division operator. In fact ideas such as int32 and int64 reveal that there are many languages that are far too bound to the hardware to be regarded as modern. Python, for example, allows arbitrary precision integer arithmetic.

All we really need is the notion of number - any precision necessary and text - any number of characters.

We might also need a Boolean type and here we get into very complicated matters with Truthy and Falsey.

The idea here is that some data values are like a false return value indicating failure. The values zero, null, undefined and the null string are falsey and they behave in logical expressions as if they were false. Everything else is truthy and they behave in logical expressions as if they were true.

This is a convention that makes some practical sense and it allows you to write things like:

```
a=a||"default value";
```

which evaluates to a if it contains any value other than zero, null, undefined or the null string and "default value" otherwise. You can see that this might be useful in applying a default value if the variable is undefined, but zero and the null string are also treated as undefined and this might not be what you want.

This viewpoint that primitive data types are irrelevant isn't particularly popular - mainly due to many years of exposure to low level languages such as C and C++ that have institutionalized the notion of primitive type. It is also true that we still occasionally need to worry about efficiency and then data representation matters.

In JavaScript and many other languages everything is an object and expressions take objects, combine them and return a new object – see Chapter-4. The operators take the appropriate "value" of each object and use it to create the new object.

From this viewpoint and in an ideal world there should be no primitive data types - just objects and operators.

Class-Based Type

Now it is time to move on to the much wider concept of type that you find in all strongly-typed, class-based languages.

Class-based type is generally what people are talking about when they discuss JavaScript and its lack of type.

We need to find out exactly what class-based typing is all about before we can look at how JavaScript copes without it.

In a class-based language declaring a class also creates a new data type.

That is:

```
Class MyClassA(){
   lots of properties
}
```

adds the new data type MyClassA to the type system.

In this system of doing things objects are of a particular type and variables have to be declared as a particular type and a variable can only reference objects of that type.

Now when you declare a variable of the type:

```
MyClassA myVariable;
```

the system knows what myVariable is referring to.

This allows the system to check that when you write:

```
myVariable.myProperty
```

that myProperty is indeed a property that is defined on the type. If it isn't then you get a compile time error which you can correct before it throws a runtime error.

Contrast this with JavaScript or any untyped language where myVariable can reference any object and hence you cannot deduce that myVariable.myProperty is valid simply by reading it. You can usually deduce its validity by reading the rest of the program, however. Strong typing makes this aspect of static analysis easier but this comes at a cost.

Notice that type occurs in two ways - a variable has a declared type and an object is of a particular type.

At its simplest the strong typing simply enforces the rule that a variable can only reference an object of its declared type.

That is, an instance of a class has a type and only a variable of the same type can reference it.

Hierarchical Typing

Things are a little more complicated in most class-based languages that implement hierarchical type. In this case inheritance can be used to create a type hierarchy.

For example:

```
Class MyClassB:inherits MyClassA{
 lots of properties
}
```

Now MyClassB has all of the properties of MyClassA plus whatever is added as part of its definition.

MyClassB is said to be a subclass of MyClassA and as it has all of the properties of MyClassA you can use it anywhere you could use an instance of MyClassA.

After all, typing is all about making sure that an object has the properties that you are using, and an instance of MyClassB has all of the properties of MyClassA and so it can be treated as such. MyClassB is also a subtype of MyClassA in the sense that it is also a MyClassA as well as being a new type all of its own.

So it is perfectly OK in most strongly-typed class-based languages to write things like:

```
MyClassA myObject=new MyClassB();
```

and then proceed to use any properties that belong to MyClassA.

So the rule has now become - a variable can reference an object of its declared type or any subtype.

If you make a mistake and try to use a property that MyClassA doesn't have, then the compiler will tell you about the error at compile time and you are saved a runtime error.

Why is hierarchical typing useful? It is useful because it allows you to write partially generic methods.

For example, suppose you have a class hierarchy Animal and two sub-classes Cat and Dog. As long as you only want to use the methods and properties of Animal you can use hierarchical typing to write a method that can accept Animal as its parameter and use it with objects of type Animal, Cat or Dog.
When you write a method that works with a type - it also works with all of its subtypes.
Most languages have a single topmost super type that all other types derive from – usually called Object or something similar. You can use this to write completely generic methods because a variable of type Object can reference anything. However, notice that because of strong typing the only methods that can be used are those that Object has.

Inheritance As the Model

Why do we use inheritance at all and why is it related to the idea of subtype?

This is a complicated question and one that causes most arguments. The original idea of using objects was to model the real world. In the real world things are objects with properties and even methods that allow the object to do something. Introducing objects into programming was to make it more like an exercise in simulation. Indeed the first object-oriented language was Simula, a language for simulation.

The idea is that in the real world objects are related to one another. The problem is that they are related in complex ways.

In programming the main intent of inheritance is to allow code reuse. If you have just spent time programming objectA and objectB is just an objectA with some extras, why not inherit all of the code from objectA into objectB. An alternative is to use copy and paste inheritance which is less efficient but achieves mostly the same results.

Code reuse doesn't have much to say about any type relationships. It is tempting to take the next step and to say that if objectB inherits from objectA then it is an objectA as well as being an objectB. A square is a square but it is also a rectangle, say. The Liskov substitution principle is the best known embodiment of this idea. This says that anywhere you can use an instance of a class, you can use an instance any sub-class. The reasoning is that the sub-class has all of the methods of the base class.

This is often true but it isn't always true.

For example, by our previous reasoning a square is a sub-class of a rectangle but you can't use a square everywhere you can use a rectangle. The reason is that you cannot set the sides of a square to different values. There is a restriction on a rectangle to make a square. Restrictions and specializations spoil the neat idea that subtypes can be used in place of their super-type. What this means is that the Liskov substitution principle is more a theoretical simplification than a reflection of the world. This also makes strong typing an arbitrary theoretical decision when it come to rules for how class instances can be used. You can find ways to make sub-classes always work as subtypes. For example if you implement a square as a rectangle that still has two sides specified, you can retain all of the rectangle methods and enforce the equality some other way. This is far from natural.

There is also the problem that in the real world objects are related to multiple other objects. A square is a special case of a rectangle and it is an n-sided equilateral shape. Some languages, notably C++, allow multiple inheritance but this creates more problems and most other languages restrict themselves to single inheritance. Other languages add to classes the idea of interfaces – essentially class declarations with no implementation. This allows for a limited form of multiple inheritance but does nothing for code reuse, forcing programmers to return to copy-and-paste code reuse.

The problem is that the real world is often not modeled well by a single inheritance hierarchy, whether used with or without strong typing. This is the main reason that you will hear advice such as "prefer composition over inheritance". The idea that one object contains another object is in many ways an easier concept to work with. So, for example, a car object might contain a steering wheel object and four road wheel objects which in turn contain wheel objects. However, this doesn't always fit, how does a square contain a rectangle object, and current languages provide poor support for composition.

JavaScript doesn't have a natural inheritance hierarchy and so cannot enforce strong typing with a type hierarchy. This doesn't mean that it cannot be used to create objects that model the real world. The idea of object-oriented programming is a good one even if inheritance and strong typing are abandoned. This also doesn't mean that you shouldn't have some mechanism for code reuse; i.e the prototype mechanism isn't a bad idea. Notice that JavaScript naturally has ways of creating mixins – objects that reuse code from multiple other objects – which provide a good alternative to multiple inheritance.

Casts

Of course you can't use properties of the subtype MyClassB when it is being referenced by a variable of type MyClassA.

In this sense it is the declared type of the variable that determines what properties are accessible and not the type of the instance the variable references.

However, there are occasions when you know that what the variable is referencing is actually a MyClassB object or more generally a subtype.

In this situation but you can use a cast or type conversion to convert something of type MyClassA into something that is of type MyClassB - as long, of course, as the object really is of that type.

So for example:

```
MyClassA myObject=new MyClassB();
```

means you can only access the properties of MyClassA via myObject, the variable's type controls what you can access, but if you write something like:

```
((MyClassB) myObject).property;
```

then property can be something defined as part of MyClassB.

That is, you have cast the myObject variable to MyClassB and overridden the restriction that the type of the variable imposes.

Notice that no "type conversion" occurs.

Type casting is all about changing the type of the variable not the object referenced.

Sometimes a cast does produce a real type conversion but this isn't a good idea. Casts and active type conversions are two different things.

A cast should just modify the type of the variable and a type conversion changes the representation of the object.

If you think this all sounds complicated - it is.

If you think this sounds all perfectly obvious, it is just because you are used to it.

Hierarchical class-based typing allows you to do many things that you could do anyway if you didn't have a type system. However, it is supposed to give you those facilities in a safe, usually said as "type safe" way.

This is fine, but typing doesn't mean you really are safe from runtime errors and some of them occur purely because because of the introduction of strong type.

For example, if you try to cast an object to a type it isn't, then you can generate a runtime error if the type isn't known and hence can't be checked at compile type.

Why do we cast?

The way that the need to cast arises is that a super-type is being used as a stand-in for one of a number of possible subtypes.

For example, if you have an Animal class which as two sub-classes Dog and Cat, then you can write a function which returns an Animal that could be either a Dog or a Cat. In any given situation you will know which it is and can cast the result to a more specific type:

```
Dog myPet=(Dog) getPet();
```

or:

```
Cat myPet=(Cat) getPet();
```

Of course this raises the question of how you know which subtype has been returned.

If you get it wrong the result is a runtime error and strong typing has let you down.

Most languages provide either a test for the type returned or a way to type convert that doesn't cause a runtime error by failing silently.

181

Overloading

There are other uses for type that look as if they are not about simply checking if an object has a given property, but in fact they are.

For example, function overloading can be used to pick which version of a function is called based on the signature of the function call.

That is, if you define two versions of a function (or method):

```
function add(int x, int y){return x+y}
```

and:

```
function add(float x, float y){return x+y}
```

then when you call add, which function is called depends on the types used to call it.

You can see that this is again a way to make sure that the code doesn't try to use properties that an object doesn't have - the right function is called to deal with the object passed.

If you think about this for a moment it is clear that the only difference between any two overridden functions is the type of the arguments. This strongly suggests that different versions are needed because of differences that come about because of the typing. In many cases function overloading is just a way of implementing generic algorithms by writing them out for each set of possible types.

Of course in JavaScript, as there is no type there can be no function overloading, but this doesn't stop you from using an operation appropriate to the object passed in. In particular by making the passed in data an object, you can always use one of its methods to do the job. For example, if int and float have an add method then the function becomes:

```
function(x,y){return x.add(y)}
```

This is, of course nothing more than a return to the principle that objects should "know" how to implement operations that involve them. In this case x "knows" what add means in its case. Of course there is always the problem that y is of a different and incompatible type but this is in the very nature of binary operations. At least x "knows" what add means and "knows" what it needs from y to implement the operation.

Polymorphism

Perhaps the best known additional use of type is polymorphism.

This is often quoted as one of the pillars of object-oriented programming and indeed it is, but the usual meaning of polymorphism goes beyond the most basic use.

Polymorphism means that when you call a method you get the method that is defined on the object.

Well at this point you might be unimpressed as what else would you expect to happen - but things are more complicated than you might expect.

When you call a method there are in fact two types involved in working out which method should be called - the variable's declared type and the object's actual type.

If a variable references an object of its declared type then obviously it should call the method defined on that type. That is:

```
MyClassA myRef=new MyClassA();
myRef.myMethod();
```

calls the myMethod defined in MyClassA. What else would it call?

Now consider MyClassB a sub-class of MyClassA and:

```
MyClassA myRef=new MyClassB();
myRef.myMethod();
```

Now the variable is declared as MyClassA but it references an object of type MyClassB.

Which myMethod should be called?

There are two possible answers.

1. The call could depend only on the declared type of the variable. That is, myMethod in MyClassA is used even though MyClassB has its own definition overriding it. The rational for this is that myRef is declared to be MyClassA and it should use the methods of MyClassA no matter what.

   This is often called a non-virtual method call and it has the advantage that it is determined at compile time. This makes it more efficient and this really is the only reason for using it.

2. The call could, and in nearly all cases should, only depend on the actual type of the object being referenced. In this case the myMethod defined in MyClassB would be used.

   This is often called a virtual method call and while it is more logical it is less efficient as the method call can only be resolved at runtime.

These two alternatives are often explained by saying that the method call can either be determined by the compile time type or the runtime type. It is more accurate to say that it is either the type of the referencing variable or the object referenced that determines the method called.

It is the virtual method call i.e. the method of the actual object type that is called that is usually referred to as polymorphism.

What possible use could this have?

The answer is that it saves having to test what to do because the action taken depends on the data - i.e. the type of the object.

The object has its own method that operates on it correctly. Instead of having to use an if statement to work out which function is appropriate, the object uses its own "function" i.e. a method to operate correctly.

The usual example of this is a class Animal which has sub-classes Dog and Cat.

If you want a function called makeSound that you can pass an Animal to i.e.:

```
makeSound(Animal pet)
```

then you will have to include an if statement in makeSound to work out what sort of animal you have been passed and issue either a woof or a meow.

However, if you give each subtype its own makeSound method which produces the correct noise for the subtype i.e. woof for Dog and meow for Cat then you don't have to test.

If the variable animal of type Animal references either a Dog or a Cat then the call:

```
animal.makeSound();
```

will give you a woof or a meow depending on whether animal references a Dog or a Cat object.

If you make use of polymorphism you get the method appropriate to the data without having to test. For this reason it is often claimed that polymorphism does away with the need to use the conditional.

What about polymorphism in JavaScript and other weakly typed languages?

In an untyped language polymorphism is the rule as variables don't have a type to use to determine the which method should be called.

The method belonging to the object referenced is always used.

Once again this is another example of the principle that an object should "know" how to perform an action on itself or appropriate to itself.

Generics

If you are familiar with a strongly-typed language then you will recount many occasions when it has picked up an error at compile time that you might have missed until runtime.

This is undoubtedly true - it happens all the time.

However, remember that what it means is that you have used the wrong object.

In this sense strong typing provides some additional "active documentation" that determines the types i.e. the objects you can use.

For every time you are saved from an error by type, you will probably have had to do some complicated dance to get around the problem that the object you have is the wrong type. In general you find that you can't just do what you want even if you know the type of the object. In particular you often can't call a method that you know that the object has, just because it is currently referenced by a variable of the wrong type.

You can decide that these benefits are worth the extra fiddle of having to cast to other types and risk runtime errors.

Many programmers do and couldn't imagine a life without strong typing.

However, strong typing also means that you cannot write generic algorithms. A generic algorithm is one that applies to a wide range of object types. For example, you might implement a sort algorithm that can sort any objects no matter what type as long as you can supply a comparison function.

There are two general ways of creating a generic method.

The first is that you can use the root of the type hierarchy, usually Object, to create variables that can reference any object type.

In most languages a variable of type Object can reference any other type in the type hierarchy - as they are all subtypes of Object. In this sense Object acts as a completely general "untyped" reference. Except, of course, as the declared type is Object you can't access any methods or properties of most of the objects it references unless you use a cast. So it isn't quite as powerful as an untyped reference.

This has the advantage of simplicity, but now you have really given up on strong typing and are using Object as a general catch-all type. You also have to rely on casting to get your data back into its real type before you can continue to use it.

The alternative is that you can use the language's generic typing facilities - if it has any. This essentially allows you to specify type as additional parameters.

Consider:

```
T add <T>(T a,T b){return a+b};
```

where <T> is a parameter that specifies the type of the object being used. When you use the generic method you have to specify the value of the type parameter.

For example:

```
int c=add<int>(1,2);
```

uses the generic method with T set to int. That is, the function declaration is:

```
int add(int a,int b){return a+b};
```

Of the two methods, generics is better because it type checks the method in the form in which you are using it. However, it is more complicated and it also has its limitations in most implementations.

For example, as the type isn't known at compile time, generally you can't use any of its methods and in this case the function given as an example would be invalid. Most languages provide a way of specifying that the type T is at least a particular class and then you can use methods.

Of course, if you drop typing then every function you write can be generic.

In fact things switch around in this case and the problem becomes not making functions work with a wide range of objects, but restricting the range that they work with.

All JavaScript functions and methods are generic.

The Final Word

When it comes to typing and type systems there is no final word.

There are arguments that strong typing creates a discipline of code that makes errors less likely, and this is true. Any discipline in coding probably produces better code. In most cases, there is no harm in adopting a strong typing approach apart from the fact that it makes some more sophisticated tasks more difficult than they need to be.

Strong typing makes simple mistakes easy to avoid, but doing sophisticated things becomes harder.

You can argue that most of the code we write isn't difficult. You can also argue that most programmers don't create huge class libraries, and therefore many of the issues of inheritance are irrelevant.

This is also true.

What is important to realize is that strong typing, based on a hierarchical type system, serves just one purpose - to check at compile time that an object you are using has the properties you are using.

Strong typing is like a straight-jacket - it keeps you sane by restricting what you can do.

The real problem here is that this is not always possible and when it isn't possible you have to resort to other approaches.

There is also the small matter that the type of an object isn't always defined at compile time. An object that is downloaded, or dynamically generated in some other way, cannot be type-checked at compile time. If it turns out to be the wrong type then you get a runtime error anyway.

In a language that is not strongly typed it is still often possible to work out if a method call or property access is valid by just looking to see if the object used supports it - this is often called type inference, but only because the world is obsessed with the idea of type.

When this cannot be determined at compile time, then the dynamic language has to resort to the same approaches as the strongly-typed language.

In the next chapter we find out about some of the ineffective ways JavaScript has been modified to try to make it more like class-based languages.

Summary

- Primitive data types are about how data is stored and this is only about efficiency.

- Differences in data are all represented in the operators and methods that can be applied to them.

- Class-based hierarchical type checking, in fact all type checking, is about answering the question - does this object support this property/method - at compile time.

- Inheritance was initially about code reuse and then turned into a way to model the supposed hierarchical nature of the real world. No single inheritance hierarchy can hope to do this.

- Hierarchical typing follows from class hierarchies and strong typing is the enforcement of the rule that a variable of a given type can only reference that type or a subtype.

- Casting is about changing what a variable can reference and not about type conversion.

- The Liskov substitution principle is an additional restriction on inheritance and often not a natural one.

- Most of the additional mechanisms, generics, polymorphism, overloading – are attempts to get back to the principle that an object should "know" how to perform an operation on itself.

- Even with strong typing it isn't always possible to determine the answer at compile time.

- Even without hierarchical inheritance and strong typing, objects are a good way to model the real world.

Chapter 12

The Search For Type

It is clear that JavaScript is a subtle and sophisticated language that deserves to be treated in its own right and not as a poor copy of other object-oriented languages.

JavaScript doesn't have type so the question is how do we cope?

Many programmers are so certain that they need a strong type system that they attempt to find it in JavaScript.

There are some facilities that seem to provide some sort of replacement for the idea of type and inheritance, and these are the subject of this chapter.

In particular we look at the constructor and its associated prototype object as substitutes for an object's type and how `instanceof` attempts to provide something like subtypes.

There are so many problems with all of these approaches that, to an extent, the purpose of this chapter is to point out how they fail so that if you use them you know what to expect.

Mostly all of the facilities in this chapter are best avoided unless you really understand them and have a use for them.

In the next chapter we look at realtime type checking and some alternatives to typing.

Prototypical Inheritance

JavaScript is usually described as using prototypical inheritance.

What this means is that every object has a prototype chain of other objects which are used to supply properties not defined on the original object.

Every object has either null or null and Object in their prototype chain. It is quite easy to construct a prototype hierarchy that looks very much like a class-based type hierarchy.

First of all, notice that you can't set a prototype object, only a prototype chain.

That is, if you set an object as the prototype object, it brings with it a prototype chain, even if this is only null.

Second, an object can only have a single prototype chain, but it can be included in many prototype chains.

This encourages programmers to think that the prototype chain is somehow something like an inheritance hierarchy, and hence presents the possibility of recovering something like class-based programming.

This isn't the case.

For example, you could have an animal object, a dog object and a cat object and the following prototype hierarchy:

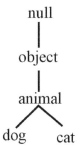

What this means is that both dog and cat have animal and object as their prototype chain.

Notice that this is an object hierarchy not a class hierarchy.

What this means is that each entity is an object. The animal object that is in the dog's and cat's prototype chains is the same object.

This means that the animal object provides all of its properties to both dog and cat unless they provide their own properties.

There are a number of differences between this and a class hierarchy.

- Although names have been given to the objects in the diagram, objects don't have names, only variables that reference them. If the animal object is also referenced by another variable called "creature" then presumably it could also be called the creature object. You can alleviate this problem by using a `const` reference, but this doesn't stop other variables with different names referencing the same object.

- If you create another animal object, i.e. an object with all the same methods and properties, then the new object would not be part of the hierarchy as drawn as it is a different object from the one labeled as animal. If the animal object is created by a constructor, say, which of the identical objects should be used as the prototype? The problem is that there is no special "animal" object that is natural to use as the super-object for dog and cat.

- Any new animal object would have the same prototype chain leading back to Object and null.

190

♦ In a class hierarchy you can create an instance of a class and expect the system to supply all of the inherited methods. For example, you could create a dog object from the Dog class without having to explicitly create an animal object first. In an object hierarchy all of the objects have to be explicitly created. For example, creating a dog object involves specifying an existing animal object as its prototype.

Perhaps the most telling difference is the lack of a fixed name associated with an object. In a class-based language you can define an Animal class and use this to stamp out lots of different instances and you would call these instances of Animal. You think of them as all being the same type of "thing". In a non-class language, objects don't have this sort of "type" identity and they don't form natural groups.

In this sense, in JavaScript every object is a singleton.

Finally, the prototype chain fails as a model of an inheritance hierarchy because it is a chain of unique objects and not a relationship between entities that create objects as in a class-based system.

This suggests that we should look more closely at the constructor which plays the role of the object creator in JavaScript.

The Constructor As An Object's "type"

Every JavaScript object is associated with two important objects - its constructor and its prototype, and both play a role in attempts to apply the ideas of type to JavaScript.

The constructor is the first related object we need to consider because a constructor usually creates multiple identical objects. In this sense a constructor creates multiple instances of the abstract object it was designed to create, and even though it is an object it plays the role of a class.

In fact this cozy picture of a constructor stamping out identical objects isn't necessarily true - but let's assume it is for the moment.

Even object literals can be considered to have Object as their constructor and Object.prototype as their prototype.

If you know an object's constructor then you know the minimum set of properties and methods an object supports, i.e. all of those added by the constructor and all of those added by the prototype chain set by the constructor.

So there is a very strong sense that the "type" of an object is related to its constructor. If you know an object's constructor then you can be fairly certain it has a given set of properties, especially if it is frozen or sealed.

Even if you allow dynamic ad-hoc properties, you can still assume that objects created by the constructor have the same minimum set of properties. It is only when you start using the delete operator that things go wrong.

However, even if you do ban the delete operator this isn't absolutely true because a constructor could conditionally add properties.

For example:

```
var C=function(){
      this.x=10;
      if(Math.random()<0.5){
        this.y=20;
      }
    }
```

This creates an object which always has a property x but only has a property y 50% of the time. So if you discover that obj has been created by C you can, delete not withstanding, safely assume that it has a property x but not that it has a property y.

Such constructors are perverse but they are still valid JavaScript.

At the end of the day knowing an object's constructor is still your best guide to what properties it should have, but it is far from perfect.

As long as you make the rule that a constructor always creates objects with the same set of properties then it seems reasonable to use the name of the constructor as if it was the object's type.

So, borrowing from class-based language jargon, we can say that:

- an object *o* constructed by *C* is an instance of *C*.

This isn't good jargon because *o* and *C* are two very different objects and to say *o* is an instance of *C* suggests that it is somehow similar but it is jargon you will find commonly used.

A much bigger problem is still that the constructor doesn't have an immutable name, only variable references.

Finding the Constructor

So how can you discover an object's constructor?

At first it seems easy - every object has a constructor property which is set to reference its constructor function - but it isn't actually this easy and it often causes lots of confusion.

There is a big problem with the constructor property in that it only references the correct constructor in a small number of situations.

What is worse is that its behavior seems to be complicated and difficult to understand.

The simplest way to follow what is happening is to discover how the constructor property is set.

Recall that when you create a function object, any function object not just a constructor, the system automatically creates a prototype property and sets this to reference the new empty object.

That is, what the system does is equivalent to:

```
var C=function(){
          . . .
       };
C.prototype={};
```

Notice that the default prototype object is created when the constructor function is defined, not when it is called.

As well as creating a default prototype object the system also creates a constructor property and sets it equal to the function. That is, what the system does is almost equivalent to:

```
var C=function(){
          . . .
       };
C.prototype={};
C.prototype.constructor=C;
```

The only subtle point that we can mostly ignore is that the constructor property is actually set on the prototype so it doesn't show as an own property. Don't worry about this for the moment, all that really matters is that you understand that the constructor property, like the prototype property, is created and initialized just once when the function is defined - and not each time it is called.

This mechanism works just fine in simple situations.

For example:

```
var A=function(){
          this.z=20;
       };
```

This function definition has resulted in a prototype property being created, referencing a new empty object, with a constructor property referencing the function object referenced by A.

You can see that this is true by accessing A.prototype.constructor, e.g.:

```
console.log(A.prototype.constructor);
```

or more simply:

```
console.log(A.constructor);
```

which displays the definition of function A.

In this case you can create an instance of A and check to see what its constructor is:

```
var a=new A();
console.log(a.constructor);
console.log(a.constructor===A);
```

You will again see the definition of function A which is indeed the constructor or object a, i.e the final instruction is true.

So in this simple case the prototype object that a constructor sets supplies the object constructed with a reference to its constructor - which is exactly what we need.

So to test if the object referenced by a has been constructed by the constructor referenced by A you would use:

```
if(a.constructor===A){
```

The condition is true if constructor and A reference the same Function object. Which is true in this case.

The constructor property correctly identifies the constructor function in this case - but it is the only case where it does.

Now consider setting your own custom prototype object:

```
var B=function(){
        this.y=20;
      };
B.prototype=new A();
```

The assignment of a prototype to B replaces the default prototype object created by the system.

What happens is almost equivalent to:

```
var B=function(){
        ...
      };
B.prototype={};
B.prototype.constructor=B;
B.prototype=new A();
```

You will notice that we have now lost the setting of the prototype's constructor property to B because we have replaced the default prototype object.

The new prototype object created using A does have a constructor property but it is set to reference function A and not the correct constructor B.

So now if you try:

```
var b=new B();
console.log(b.constructor===B);
```

you will find that the result is false.

You will also find that:

```
console.log(b.constructor===A);
```

is true. The reason is that b doesn't have a constructor property and the first prototype in the chain, i.e. the new instance of A, doesn't have a constructor property but its prototype does and this is set by the system to A.

Because the constructor property is only set for the default prototype object, it doesn't get updated correctly when you override this with some other prototype object, and overriding is what you have to do if you want to build up a prototype chain.

As a result, in any prototype chain the constructor property can only be set correctly for the first object in the prototype chain, and then only if it is the default prototype object created by the constructor.

This is the reason why it is often said that the constructor property gives the constructor, not of the object, but of the object's prototype.

This is certainly true in this case but it is only because the prototype chain is just two objects long (ignoring Object.prototype and null).

If you try:

```
var C=function(){
        this.x=30;
    };
C.prototype=new B();
var c=new C();
console.log(c.constructor===C);
console.log(c.constructor===B);
console.log(c.constructor===A);
```

You will discover that the constructor property is set to A and not B as it should be if it was the constructor of C's immediate prototype and not C if it was the constructor of c.

It is set to A - the constructor of the first object in the prototype chain and not the constructor of C's prototype i.e. B. The rule is that by default the constructor property gives the constructor of the first prototype in the chain as long as it hasn't been explicitly set to an object.

You can fix this default behavior by explicitly setting the constructor property each time you supply your own custom prototype object:

```
var A=function(){
        this.z=20;
 };
var a=new A();
console.log(a.constructor===A);

var B=function(){
        this.y=20;
 };
B.prototype=new A();
B.prototype.constructor=B;
var b=new B();
console.log(b.constructor===B);

var C=function(){
        this.x=30;
      };
C.prototype=new B();
C.prototype.constructor=C;
var c=new C();
console.log(c.constructor===C);
```

You will now find that each object does have a constructor property, supplied by its prototype, that does give the correct constructor.

You can even work your way down the prototype chain finding each constructor in turn:

```
console.log(C.prototype.constructor === C);
console.log(C.prototype.prototype.constructor === B);
console.log(C.prototype.prototype.prototype.constructor === A);
```

Notice that we are walking the prototype chain as defined by the constructors. We could do the same thing using the object via the getPrototypeOf method.

So problem solved - as long as you remember to do the bookkeeping because JavaScript doesn't do it for you except in the case of a default prototype object. The only problem is that many beginners think that the constructor property "just works" - it doesn't.

To be precise:

   ◆ If you want to make use of the constructor property to track the "type" of an object you have to remember to set it yourself.

The Mystery of Instanceof - Subtype

Knowing what type an object is isn't the end of the story.

In a class-based language the type hierarchy means that it is possible to consider an object as being of a number of different types and subtypes.

For example, every object is an instance of Object as well as whatever class it actually is.

If class B inherits from class A then an instance of class B can be considered to be a class A instance as well as it having all of the properties and methods of an instance of class A.

This is the Liskov substitution principle and it applies, with some exceptions due to dynamic properties, in JavaScript. See the previous chapter for a full discussion.

For example, if an object d has a prototype chain:

```
c → b → a → Object.prototype → null
```

then it is not only an instance of D but it can also be treated as an instance of C, B or A.

With this explained we can now understand the intention of the instanceof operator.

The instanceof operator looks as if it is a way of testing to see if an object was constructed by a particular constructor, but this isn't what it does at all.

It is often explained that we can test to see if obj has constructor C using:

```
obj instanceof C;
```

which will return true if obj was constructed by C.

This looks as if it is just an alternative to testing an object's constructor property, but again this is not what it is doing.

The instanceof operator doesn't check the constructor but the prototype that the constructor specifies.

That is:

```
obj instanceof C:
```

compares the object's prototype to the prototype specified in the constructor. If they are the same then it might seem reasonable to conclude that obj was constructed by C.

But things are a little more complicated than this simple introduction suggests.

Not only does instanceof test to see if the prototype the constructor specifies is the immediate prototype of the object, it also checks to see if the prototype is anywhere in the object's complete prototype chain.

So to be 100% clear:

```
obj instanceof C;
```

looks for C.prototype in the object's entire prototype chain and returns true if it finds it.

Instanceof doesn't test that the object was created by the constructor you specify. It tests if the object has the prototype specified by the constructor anywhere in the object's prototype chain.

So if obj instanceof C is true you can't conclude that C was the object's constructor. All you can conclude is that object has a specific prototype object P in its prototype chain and hence it has all of the properties of P.

You could say that the statement:

```
obj instanceof C
```

being true lets you conclude that obj is of type P, where P is the prototype object specified by C.

For example consider the following:

```
var p={x:10};

var A=function(){
        this.z=20;
    };
A.prototype=p;

var B=function(){
        this.y=30;
    };
B.prototype=p;
```

We have defined two different constructors A and B with the same prototype p.

That is the inheritance branches:

Notice that A and B construct objects with different sets of properties - an instance of A has x and z, and an instance of B has x and y.

Now if you create an object using B:

```
var b=new B();
```

and test using instanceof:

```
console.log(b instanceof A);
```

you will discover that b is an instance of A (i.e. the result is true) even though it was created by B.

You can also see that there is no reasonable sense in which b is an instance of A - it only shares the same prototype with objects created by A. In this sense it would be more reasonable to say that b was a p.

So why did anyone add instanceof to JavaScript?

If you restrict yourself to a strictly non-branching inheritance structure then instanceof does sort of work.

If you change the previous example to one in which B "inherits" from A then it makes a little more sense:

```
var p={x:10};
var A=function(){
        this.z=20;
      };
A.prototype=p;
var B=function(){
        this.z=30;
      };
B.prototype=new A();
```

You can see that now we have an inheritance with no branches given by:

```
b → a → p → object.prototype → null
```

i.e. any object created by B has all of the properties of one created by A and both have all of the properties of p.

Now if you create an instance of B:

```
var b=new B();
```

then:

```
console.log(b instanceof A);
```

is true because b has p in its prototype chain and because the inheritance is hierarchical it also has all of the properties of A. Notice also that in this case an A would not be considered to be an instance of a B because B's prototype is A and A is not in A's prototype chain.

As long as you stick to a strict hierarchical non-branching"inheritance" using prototypes then the `instanceof` operator gives you the results you might expect.

If the inheritance branches, as most do, then you get a seemingly wrong answer from `instanceof` if you regard it as telling you about constructors.

Where Are We?

JavaScript provides two "helper" functions for programmers wanting to reinvent type, but they both are very deeply flawed.

Knowing what an object's constructor is does specify what properties it has, and so it is a reasonable interpretation of type. The problem is that the constructor property, which is supplied by the prototype object, is only set automatically for the default prototype object.

If you supply a prototype object of your own to build up a prototype chain, then you have to remember to set its constructor property to reference the constructor.

This can be made to work, but it isn't ideal and it is just one of many manual schemes you could implement that track the "type" of an object.

Knowing that a particular object, p say, is in an object's prototype chain, lets you treat the object as if it was an instance of p, i.e. its subtype is P.

The `instanceof` operator doesn't check that an object is an instance of a particular constructor, i.e. was created by the constructor as its name suggests. It simply checks to see if the prototype specified by the constructor is in the object's prototype chain. Hence it checks if the object is a subtype P, the same as the prototype specified by the constructor.

The problem with the `instanceof` operator is that it seems to be checking for one thing and it actually checks, imperfectly, for another. However, the basic idea that a prototype being in an object's prototype chain determines a sort of analog of subtype is a good one. This idea shouldn't be thrown out along with the broken attempt at an `instanceof` operator.

It is clear that with the current model of prototype inheritance, the best analog of type is the constructor, and the best analog of subtype is the prototype chain.

However, at the start of the chapter it was suggested that trying to find an analog of class-based type might not be a good idea at all and, if it is, then perhaps constructor/prototype definitions are not the way to go.

In the next chapter we meet duck testing as an alternative to trying to reinvent class-based type.

Summary

- The constructor is the best analog of type in JavaScript.

- The prototype chain provides an analog of subtype.

- The constructor property only works for the default prototype object.

- If you supply a custom prototype then you have to set the constructor property.

- The `instanceof` operator doesn't test for an instance of the specified constructor. It checks the prototype chain for the occurrence of the prototype specified by the constructor.

- There are probably better ways of dealing with the lack of type in JavaScript.

Chapter 13

Property Checking

Attempts to impose type on JavaScript just don't seem to work unless you turn JavaScript into a completely different language and lose many of its advantages.

As we discussed in previous chapters, the invention of strong typing, based on the class hierarchy that results from single inheritance, is an elegant idea. So elegant that it is difficult to see what its disadvantages are. It is an unarguable fact that it catches errors at compile time that might otherwise go unnoticed until runtime. However, these errors are simple static errors that are easy to pick up without strong typing.

You might well argue that as strong typing is so simple to implement, even if it only picks up static errors perhaps it is a good way to do the job. It isn't. The reason is that strong typing imposes a set of restrictions that we have to invent increasingly complex ways to overcome. Static typing means you can't write generic functions without inventing generics and all of its complications of variance and so on. If you know that a variable is referencing a subtype, then to make use of the subtype's methods you have to cast to that subtype. This sounds mysterious and complicated but all it does is change the type of the variable so as to allow those properties to be used. This causes additional problems that have to be solved by the introduction of introspection and metadata.

One of the problem is that attempts to find ways of making JavaScript look like a strongly-typed language have made matters worse not better.

There is an alternative to trying to reinvent type in JavaScript. As the only purpose of establishing the type of an object is to be sure what properties it has - why not forget type and concentrate on the properties with duck testing.

That is, if you can check that an object has the properties of a duck, then you can treat it like a duck.

In some situations this is by far the best thing to do but occasionally the need to test many properties becomes unwieldy and we need a better way.

Once again it is time to go back to the role of prototype inheritance which can be used to test for the possession of large sets of properties very efficiently.

Strong Typing is Property Checking

The key idea is that the only issue that strong typing is about is checking that an object has a particular set of properties. In this case we are using the term property to mean data or function properties i.e. methods.

If you include the rule that a variable of a particular type can be used to reference any subtypes as well as the type then you could say it is about checking that an object has at least a given set of properties.

If in a strongly-typed language I declare a variable to be of type String then I can use any properties that the String class declares. If I use any property that isn't declared in the String class then this is obvious at compile or editing time and it can be flagged as an error for the programmer to correct.

Type is all about characterizing the properties an object has.

If this is the case, then first we should think about how objects acquire properties in JavaScript.

How Do Objects Get Properties?

If you want to find out if an object has a property it is first a good idea to know how objects get properties.

There are four general ways:

1. static literal definition of properties:

    ```
    var obj={a:1,b:2};
    ```

2. dynamic ad hoc properties:

    ```
    obj.c=3
    ```

3. Constructor or object factory:

    ```
    var obj=new Obj();
    ```

4. via a prototype:

    ```
    Obj.prototype=new Obj2();
    var obj=new Obj();
    ```

You can argue that these are minor variations, after all a constructor will use literal and dynamic property creation. The important point is when you ask the question where did this property come from, you can usually answer it with one of the four. The static literal definition, the constructor and the prototype group together the creation of properties into one place in your program. You can read the literal definition, the constructor and the prototype and know that they add the set of properties that you can see.

Dynamic ad hoc properties are more troublesome because they can be added anywhere in your program. An object can simply accrete properties as the program progresses. This is a bad idea and good program construction should follow the rule that objects should be constructed in one place unless there is a very good reason not to.

You can forbid the dynamic addition or removal of properties using either seal or freeze and as long as you can assume that they are supported this greatly simplifies the problem.

The point is that you can find out what properties an object has by reading the code and this is what type inference is all about. However, it is important to realize that it is only called type inference because it was in the beginning implemented as a way of introducing type back into a language that doesn't use it. It would be much better to think of it as property inference.

So this is how an object can acquire a property, but in JavaScript an object can also have a property removed. The delete operator can delete any property.

Note: delete does not delete variables only properties.

The delete operator can change an object at any point in the program. It is a good idea not to use it unless you have no choice. Not allowing its use is one of the few good features of strict mode.

Compile/Edit Time Type Testing?

In a class-based language much of the type checking occurs at compile time and this provides a measure of protection at runtime. You can view type checking as a way of moving errors from runtime to compile time.

As explained earlier, what is happening in type checking is that a variable has a type and we simply check that the object it references has the same type or is a subtype.

For example, if you declare a variable to be of one type, and you try and make it reference an incompatible type you will generate a compiler error:

```
MyClass myvar=new SomeOtherClass();
```

Assuming that SomeOtherClass isn't a subclass of MyClass then this program will never get to run because the compiler will throw up a type error. Of course, if the variable wasn't typed there would be no error, and perhaps SomeOtherClass is what the programmer intended to use as it has the one important property that the programmer uses.

In the same way in a class-based language any attempt to use a property that isn't defined within the declared type is flagged up at compile time. For example:

```
String mystring=new String("Hello World"):
mystring.random();
```

will never get to run because the compiler will complain that a String doesn't have a random method (assuming it doesn't of course).

There is no compile stage for JavaScript, and what is more variables aren't typed.

So the first typical error i.e. assigning the wrong type to a variable, can't happen at any time.

However, the second common error does happen in JavaScript and it can't be flagged at compile time because there is no compile time. Instead if you run the JavaScript equivalent:

```
var mystring=new String("Hello World");
mystring.random();
```

You will see a runtime error telling you that random is an undefined property and not a function.

Many errors that are detected at compile time in class-based languages are detected at runtime in JavaScript.

This doesn't mean that they couldn't be detected at edit time – it's just that most of us don't use tools that would do the job. A static analyzer would easily pick up that mystring was referencing a String object, and a String object doesn't have a random method. You don't need to run the program and you don't need to type the mystring variable.

Runtime Type Testing

Sometimes it isn't possible to know the type the object being referenced.

The most common example is when you create a function.

For example:

```
function doSomething(x){
  x.myMethod();
}
```

What is x?

Clearly the problem is that the function cannot be checked at the point is it declared. If x was explicitly typed then the compiler or editor could check that an object of that type had a myMethod property.

Is this a clear advantage of typing?

In a non-typed language like JavaScript we have to wait until the function is used to do any checking.

For example:

```
doSomething(o);
```

only at this point can the compiler/editor check that o is an object that has a myMethod. This is also a check that the compiler has to perform in a strongly-typed language – so what was the point of the check when the function was declared? The only advantage is that it decouples the function declaration from its use. You can check that the function is correct without seeing how it is used and this is an advantage, but now you can only pass into the function objects of a single type and/or subtype. In the untyped case all that matters is that the object has a myMethod property.

Of course there are some errors are not detectable at compile/edit time because the type of the object being referenced really isn't determined until runtime i.e. the type is dynamic and in this case the only possibility is runtime detection.

Random sources of objects are far less commonly encountered, but they can be created both in strongly-typed languages and JavaScript.

For example:

```
if(math.random()>0.5){
   x=new A();
}else{
   x=new B();
};
myFunc(x);
```

If myFunc expects x to be an A then the program will crash 50% of the time.

Notice that this code can be written in a strongly-typed language using Object as a type that can be used to reference any type and by making myFunc cast x to an A:

```
if(rand>0.5){
 object x=new A();
}else{
 object x=new B();
}
myFunc((A)x);
```

where (A)x is a cast to type A.

A more realistic situation is when an object is provided by another program but this too is less common.

The only solution in this situation is to resort to runtime testing.

Forget Type - Use Duck Testing

If you have reached this point and feel that something is lacking in trying to recreate type in JavaScript then you might like to consider the alternative - duck testing.

This idea is core to JavaScript's approach to objects which is often summed up in the old saying:

If it walks like a duck and quacks like a duck then it is a duck.

You could say more accurately that it is enough of a duck for our purposes.

If you want to check if an object has a set of properties then why not just test to see if it has - i.e. test to see if it quacks.

That is, if you can check that an object has the properties of a duck, then you can treat it like a duck.

This is very easy, works without complication and works at runtime.

For example, suppose you are passed an object and you want to use the property prop. If prop hasn't been defined on the object or its prototype chain then:

```
obj.prob
```

is undefined so you can test:

```
if(obj.prop===undefined) then object isn't usable
```

This is easy and unless you are testing lot of properties repeatedly it is efficient. If you are checking lots of properties repeatedly just do it once and set a validated property so that you don't do it again.

There is one additional problem; the property might exist i.e. might be defined, but it might have the wrong type of value.

This usually occurs when you do something like this:

```
if(obj.method!==undefined) alert(obj.method());
```

only to discover a runtime exception because method isn't a function object and so cannot be called.

This is where primitive type enters the picture.

JavaScript may not be strongly-typed but it does recognize the need to know what sort of object you are working with.

Testing Primitive Type - typeof

The typeof operator will return a string that gives the primitive type of an object.

Mozilla lists the following results for typeof:

Type	Result
Undefined	`"undefined"`
Null	`"object"`
Boolean	`"boolean"`
Number	`"number"`
String	`"string"`
Symbol (new in ECMAScript 6)	`"symbol"`
Host object (provided by the JS environment)	*Implementation-dependent*
Function object (implements [[Call]] in ECMA-262 terms)	`"function"`
Any other object	`"object"`

This seems reasonable apart from perhaps Null being an object.

Unfortunately, not all browsers implement the strict definition of a function object as something you can call. In particular Chrome to version 12 defined a regular expression as a function.

Using typeof you can test to see not only that a property exists but that it is of the correct primitive type.

For example:

```
if(typeof(obj.method)==="function") alert("it is a function");
```

This tests that obj.method exists and that it is a function. If it doesn't exist typeof returns the string "undefined".

As most of the time you are only concerned about the distinction between property and method, this is the most useful of duck tests. Notice, however, that you still have to check that obj is defined to avoid an exception.

If you are going to test a set of properties on an object then one approach is to define a null object if you find it undefined:

```
if(obj===undefined) var obj={};
if(typeof(obj.method)==="function") alert("it is a function");
```

This relies on you testing each method and property before using it.

An alternative and slightly more secure method for a Function object is to test first to see if the property exists and then test to see if the constructor is what you expect.

For example:

```
if(obj.method!==undefined){
  alert(obj.method.constructor===Function);
};
```

This first tests that method exists and then that it is a function by checking the constructor.

You can use this method for general objects where you set a custom constructor as long as you always remember to set the constructor property.

Trying the Duck

OK, so you know that the property exists.

You know that it is the right sort of property.

It can still all go horribly wrong.

A function might not have the right parameters and it might not return the correct sort of thing.

Fortunately as JavaScript doesn't insist on a fixed number of parameters and handles untyped returns, misusing a function doesn't result in a runtime error unless the function itself crashes.

You could check each of the parameters and even the return type but if you don't know where the object came from it could be completely broken even though all of the surface detail checks out.

Perhaps the simplest way to implement duck testing is to simply put the whole of the property access inside a try-catch.

For example:

```
try{
  obj.func();
}
catch(ex){
  alert("problem with this object");
}
```

This catches all of the possible problems with the property access including things that type checking couldn't possibly get.

Of course there are some problems with this approach.

The first is that try catch statements slow code down - not by much but they make optimization harder. This probably means you should keep such checking outside of loops - check a property access once.

Another problem is more theoretical. Exceptions that are handled by try-catch really should be exceptions and not just logical conditions that you are too lazy to test for. However, in this case if your worry is that the object that you have been passed is in some way faulty, then using an exception is reasonable.

Try-catch really does seem like the total solution to the problem with only minor disadvantages.

If you cannot determine the type of object a variable references at runtime, then it is reasonable to enclose any use of its properties in a try-catch.

Of course this doesn't tell you what you should do when you discover that you have the wrong type of object - but this is a problem common to all languages.

Prototype Testing - getPrototypeOf and isPrototypeOf

Duck testing individual properties is fine, but sometimes you just want to check that an object supports a block of properties.

In the previous chapter the idea of testing to see if a particular object was in the prototype chain was introduced via the strange instanceof operator.

The idea is that you can treat an object as a bag of properties and if you know that a particular object is in the prototype chain you can reasonably rely on its properties being available.

In ES5 there are two new features which make prototype chain testing much easier and much more direct.

Until ES5 there was no way to discover an object's immediate prototype but now you can use the getPrototypeOf(obj) method to directly access the internal prototype property of any object.

Notice that getPrototypeOf returns a reference to the prototype object.

So if an object d has a prototype chain given by:

```
c → b → a → Object.prototype → null
```

then:

```
var d=new D();
console.log(Object.getPrototypeOf(d));
```

will display the properties of c. A common way of saying this is that d is a subtype of c or even that d is an instance of c, but it is much better to just say that d has all of the properties of c.

Put simply, stop worrying about type and just focus on the fact that d has all of the properties of c and you can make use of them without further testing.

This is very handy, but in most cases you are not just interested in the immediate prototype. You really don't care where an object is in the prototype chain, you usually just want to know that it is in the prototype chain. You could use getPrototypeOf to walk the prototype chain e.g.:

```
console.log(Object.getPrototypeOf(
                  Object.getPrototypeOf(d)));
```

returns an instance of B, but why bother when there is isPrototypeOf(obj).

This will test to see if the prototype is in the prototype chain of obj.

For example:

```
proto.isPrototypeOf(obj);
```

is true if the object proto is in the prototype chain of obj.

The main problem with using isPrototypeOf is getting a reference to the prototype object in the first place.

So if you have a prototype chain:

```
c → b → a → Object.prototype → null
```

then:

```
var d=new D();
console.log(b.isPrototypeOf(d));
```

will be true is b is in the prototype chain of d.

Notice that in this case for this to be true b has to be a reference to the instance that is actually part of the prototype chain. You can't simply create a new instance of B. That is you can't simply do:

```
var C=function(){
        this.x=30;
      };
C.prototype=new B();
```

and then:

```
var d=new D();
var b=new B();
console.log(b.isPrototypeOf(d));
```

The instance of B that is the prototype isn't the same instance as referenced by b. It isn't enough that the objects are of the same "type" they have to be the same object.

JavaScript works with objects and every "instance" no matter how similar is a completely different object.

What you have to do is keep a reference to the prototype when you create it. For example:

```
var C=function(){
 this.x=30;
};
var b=new B();
C.prototype=b;
```

Now you can do:

```
var d=new D();
console.log(b.isPrototypeOf(d));
```

and the result will be true.

Another common pattern is the use of a constructor's prototype property to see if its prototype is in the object's prototype chain:

```
var d=new D();
console.log(B.prototype.isPrototypeOf(d));
```

In this case it is tempting to interpret a true result as indicating that B is d's constructor but this is obviously not the case. All it indicates is that the prototype of B is in d's prototype chain.

Prototype Chain Checking Problems

At this point you have the machinery to check that any particular object is in the prototype chain.

This at first seems to be very useful.

If it so happens that your design lends itself to a hierarchical structure with each new object inheriting from the objects that came before, and each object elaborating on the basic object, then you can write functions that accept an object from any point in the hierarchy down - just as you can in a class-based language.

To use an old and completely unrealistic example suppose you have an animal object and dog and cat objects which have animal in their prototype chain, and a kitten and puppy objects which have cat and dog objects as their prototype respectively.

That is the chains are:

```
kitten cat → animal → Object → null
puppy  dog → animal → Object → null
```

This is perfect hierarchical inheritance and you can write a function that demands that the object is an instance of an animal i.e. has all of the properties of an animal object using:

```
 var myfunction(obj){
 if(!animal.isPrototypeOf(obj))return:
  ..
```

This will accept any cat, kitten, puppy or dog object and as long as you only use methods that are defined in animal it all works.

However, do you notice another problem?

This method doesn't accept an animal object even though you would expect it to because animal has all of the properties you are testing for in the other objects.

The reason is, of course, that animal isn't part of its own prototype chain. Its properties are defined as own properties in the animal object.

To test animal or any subtype of animal you have to test that animal is in the prototype chain or the constructor was Animal.

This is messy but can be done, as long as you remember to always set the constructor property on each of the prototypes, either the constructor or in the prototype chain.

The problem is that when you use a constructor in the usual way the object itself isn't regarded as part of its own prototype chain and so you have to test for it separately.

A much better solution is to use a prototype constructor approach.

The Prototype Constructor

We have already seen that there are advantages to placing all of the methods of an object in one of its prototypes. Although the conventional wisdom suggests that there should be a split between methods and data properties, this isn't necessarily the case. The argument is that data properties should always be instance properties because this is logical and methods should be prototype methods because this is efficient.

However, if you are using the prototype chain to test for the availability of a set of properties then this is easier and more logical if all of the properties, both data and methods, are prototype properties. In this case the constructor is only used to establish the prototype and in many cases it can be dispensed with.

● That is all of the properties of the constructed object are supplied by the prototype - hence prototype constructor.

You can think of the empty object that the constructor creates as waiting to be used to store any properties that have to be promoted to own properties. This is an example of the copy on write principle, because something is stored in them. The empty object can also be used to store any dynamic properties that are created as the program runs.

In other words, the prototype holds all of initial properties of the object created by A and the prototype completely defines the object created by the constructor.

This is a very simple and yet powerful idea - put everything that defines an object in the prototype, why not?

This is the idea of a prototype constructor and it makes object construction very easy. It is also a natural fit with the idea that the prototype chain defines subtype and type.

It also overcomes the problem introduced in the previous section because now the object being constructed is always part of its prototype chain.

For example, to create the previous object complete with sum function you would use:

```
var A = function() { };
A.prototype.x = 1;
A.prototype.y = 2;
A.prototype.sum = function() {
                    return(this.x + this.y);
                };
```

Notice that the constructor doesn't do a thing, its all in the prototype and there is only ever one instance of the prototype object:

```
var a = new A();
alert(a.sum());
```

In this case the sum method and the values of x and y are provided by the prototype. If you assign to x or y then it becomes an own property and isn't supplied by the prototype:

```
a.x=2;
alert(a.sum());
```

Notice also that if you want the new object to have a more complex prototype chain you can add:

```
A.prototype=Object.create({},proto);
```

where proto is the object at the head of the desired prototype chain, before adding properties to the prototype.

If you don't like the untidy way that creating the prototype is outside of a function you can wrap all of the prototype constructors inside an immediately invoked function that returns the constructor:

```
var A = (function() {
            var temp = function() { };
            temp.prototype.x = 1;
            temp.prototype.y = 2;
            temp.prototype.sum = function() {
                                    return(this.x + this.y);
                                };
            return temp;
        })();

var a = new A();
alert(a.x);
alert(a.sum());
```

This looks complicated but is always follows the same form. Create and return a function, the constructor that does nothing and use its prototype to define the object.

Note once again that no matter how many instances A creates they all share the same prototype chain. The only new object created when you create an instance of A is a new empty object {} which is waiting to store any instance/own properties that are created when you store a value in a prototype property.

How does prototype inheritance work if you use a prototype constructor?

It all works very naturally. Let's create a B constructor that inherits from A:

```
var B = (function() {
        var temp=function(){};
        temp.prototype = new A();
        temp.prototype.z = 2;
        return temp ;
     })();
```

We now just create an instance of A to act as the prototype. If you think about it for a moment, an instance of A is an empty object with a prototype that provides its properties. So we are back to where we started with an empty object that we can add properties to as necessary to create a derived object. In this case we simply add a z property.

This only works correctly if A is constructed entirely via its prototype. Also notice that all instances of B share the same prototype object and hence the complete prototype chain as before; the only new object created is an empty object ready to store any own properties.

You can try this out with:

```
var b = new B();
alert(b.sum());
alert(b.z);
```

and you will see that b has properties provided by its prototype and the earlier prototype.

You can also add the setting of the constructor property on the prototype, but this isn't particularly useful.

The point is that the object being constructed is always the first prototype in the prototype chain, and not the empty object returned by the constructor, so you really don't need to know what the constructor is.

So, for example, the B constructor creates an empty object {} with the following prototype chain:

```
{} → b → a → object.prototype → null
```

That is you can determine both type and subtype using nothing but isPrototypeOf.

For example:

```
B.prototype.isPrototypeOf(b);
```

is true and can be interpreted to mean that b is an instance of B.

As you can now regard an object as being in its prototype chain it solves the problem of the last section where testing for things that inherit from animal didn't include the animal object itself.

We also have:

```
A.prototype.isPrototypeOf(b);
```

is also true and this can be interpreted to mean that b is also an instance of A i.e. a subtype of A. This approach also makes the otherwise strange instanceof operator work as it should.

For example:

```
b instanceof B;
```

is true and this really does mean that b has all of the properties of an object constructed by B. Of course it works because it it exactly equivalent to:

```
B.prototype.isPrototypeOf b;
```

Both also work correctly when the inheritance hierarchy branches.

For example, if you create a C that also inherits from A:

```
var C =( function() {
        var temp=function(){};
        temp.prototype = new A();
        temp.prototype.z = 2;
        return temp ;
    })();
```

```
var c=new C();
```

then:

```
c instanceof A;
c instanceof C;
```

are both true but:

```
c instanceof B;
```

is false which is what you would expect - but compare with the same example in the previous chapter where things don't work as expected.

Using the prototype constructor approach makes instanceof work correctly and allows you to test for the type and subtype using just the prototype chain.

An even better way to organize the prototype chain is to use singleton objects to be representative objects of the objects the constructor creates. This makes it clear that all of the instances relate back to the relevant prototype objects and makes it easier to think about.

Testing

You might be thinking that we are missing out on an advantage of strong typing by having to include runtime tests in our code. Do we really have to test that an object has a particular property every time the program is run?

If the object and property are only determined at runtime then the answer is yes, and it is yes even if a language supports strong typing.

The only situation where you are saved a runtime test is when the object is determined before runtime. In this case you can include a test for the object and property in the code but it is only ever needed once. Once the code passes the test it will always pass the test.

At this point you should be thinking of unit testing or even test driven development. A testing engine will add tests to your code that you can run just once when you are determining if it passes all tests in the test suite. The tests are removed from your production code.

There are a number of testing frameworks for JavaScript but QUnit, from the people who brought you jQuery, is simple and powerful enough for most purposes. QUnit makes no modifications to your production JavaScript and the only requirement is that it is stored in a file separate from the HTML in the project. You load the code into a testing module and then the tests are executed to verify that the code passes the tests. It is very easy to set up tests for each object and method to ensure that it works with the required types and that it does the correct thing with the required types.

You can find out more about QUnit in my book *Just jQuery: The Core UI ISBN:978-1871962505.*

Runtime Testing

Most of the time you can ignore issues of "type" because JavaScript objects generally don't use complex prototype chains and hardly use concepts such as inheritance.

Most of the time you don't even have to do runtime duck testing because the code sets the object in such away that it cannot fail.

Put simply, the most common situation is that if the code works just once it will always work.

You can think of this sort of runtime error as a deterministic error because if you don't correct it then it will always happen.

For example if you write:

```
var a=new A();
```

then it is clear that a references an object constructed by A. If you then go on and use just the properties of A then the code will run. If it doesn't you need to correct what would be a compile time type error in a strongly-typed language. If you don't correct the error then it will happen every time you run the program.

Even when you write a function with a untyped parameter in JavaScript:

```
var myFunc=function(x){...};
```

then there are many situations where if the program works once it will always work.

For example, if the function uses x as if it was an a and the code is:

```
var a=new A();
function(a);
```

There just isn't enough variability in the code for it to subsequently fail if it works even once. Looking at it another way, a static type error is easy to find and easy to correct as long as you make sure that all of the code you have written is executed i.e. this is an issue of code coverage in testing.

To make it easier to write code that doesn't fail at runtime, the IDE usually can provide some help. Class-based languages often have editors that give you hints about what properties an object has. They can do this because the class that defines the object is essentially an inventory of its properties.

JavaScript IDEs can do the same thing by deducing the properties that an object has. For example in NetBeans if you enter a constructor:

```
var A=function(){
        this.x=10;
        this.y=20;
};
```

then the Navigator pane shows the constructor object and its properties as if it was a class.

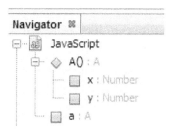

When you start to use an object constructed by A NetBeans will offer you a list of properties that you can select from.

```
35    a.|
36    ☐ x: Number
37    ☐ y: Number
38    ☐ constructor: Function
39    ☐ length: Number
40    ◯ apply(thisArg: String, argArray: Object)..
41    ◯ bind(thisArg: Object): String
      ◯ call(thisArg: Object): String
      ◉ create(O: Object): Object
Output ⌘  ◉ defineProperties(O: Object, Properties: ..
```

This is usually referred to as type inference, but what is going on is the inference of the object and its properties that a variable references.

Of course, there are lots of places where this goes wrong. For example, and this is the most common and worrying, when you write a function there is no way for the IDE to work out the properties of any of the parameters.
That is, in:

```
function(x){...}
```

x really is unknown.

At this point people often suggest that annotation is the solution, but this is simply reinventing type. A better solution might be to have a facility to simply tell the IDE the expected type of the variable using an interactive UI.

There are a number of static code analysis applications that have the ability to use type inference to help you find runtime bugs before they happen. You can use ESLint, Flow, tern and even TypeScript to parse your JavaScript and improve it, but most such programs expect you to modify your code with type annotations. This is not a small matter. It changes your workflow from interactive to something more akin to a traditional compile-execute cycle. It also changes your code from pure JavaScript that can run unmodified into something that isn't JavaScript. For example, Flow, a type inference engine from Facebook, demands that you use the Babel compiler to remove any type annotations. While this might seem like a safe thing to do now, who knows how long the applications concerned will remain current.

Summary

- JavaScript doesn't have a compile time and doesn't have type, so all of the checks that would often be done by compile time type checking have to be performed at runtime.

- Duck testing is the simplest approach to ensuring that an object has the properties you want to use.

- Use `typeof` to determine primitive type when necessary.

- Use try-catch to ensure that a method does what you expect.

- You can use `getPrototypeOf` and `isPrototypeOf` to test a prototype chain for the presence of an object that acts in place of type. However, this doesn't work well because an object is not part of its own prototype chain.

- Using prototype constructors, which always return an empty object with an extended prototype chain, solves all of the problems in using `getPrototypeOf` and `isPrototypeOf`.

- You can add a single object to the prototype chain of an existing object to create an "interface-like" mechanism by adding to the front of the chain.

- Tools can help with writing correct JavaScript without the need to modify the language and without the need to give up the advantages of an untyped dynamic language.

Index

225